DOUBLE DOWN

A Guide to the Best of Vegas Limestone & Sandstone

Introduction

Double Down: A Guide to the Best of Vegas Limestone & Sandstone

©2006 by Sharp End Publishing. All rights reserved. This book or any part thereof may not be reproduced in any form whatsoever, other than for brief passages embodied in critical reviews or articles, without permission of the publisher.

ISBN   1-892540-23-1

Front Cover Photos: Jared McMillan on Countdown To Armageddon at Mt. Charleston (photo by Jorge Visser) and Liv Sansoz on Fear and Loathing at The Gallery (photo by Olivier Appourchaux)

Photo on previous page: Christa Hollenberg on Running Man at The Gallery (photo: Jorge Visser)

Printed in the United States of America.

For more information or to order books contact:
Sharp End Publishing   (303) 444-2698
P.O. Box 1613   www.sharpendbooks.com
Boulder, CO 80306-1613

READ THIS BEFORE USING THIS GUIDE BOOK

Rock climbing is extremely dangerous. A small and incomplete list of possible dangers includes: loose rock, weather, anchor failure (fixed anchors, natural anchors, and removable protection), dangerous pendulums, equipment failure, etc.

THE AUTHOR AND PUBLISHER EXPRESSLY DISCLAIM ALL REPRESENTATIONS AND WARRANTIES REGARDING THIS GUIDE, THE ACCURACY OF THE INFORMATION CONTAINED HEREIN, AND THE RESULTS OF YOUR USE HEREOF, INCLUDING WITHOUT LIMITATION, IMPLIED WARRANTIES OF MERCHANTABILITY AND FITNESS FOR A PARTICULAR PURPOSE. THE USER ASSUMES ALL RISK ASSOCIATED WITH THE USE OF THIS GUIDE.

It is your responsibility to take care of yourself while climbing. Seek a professional instructor or guide if you are unsure of your ability to handle any circumstances that may arise. This guide is not intended as an instructional manual.

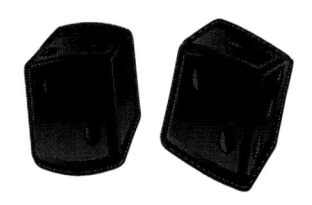

INTRODUCTION

Las Vegas is the City of Perpetual Gratification. Whatever you want you can get—and that goes for the climbing too. Vegas has just about every type of climbing one could "jones" for: trad, sport, mixed, ice, hard, easy, steep, slabby, bouldering and big walls. You just gotta know where to look.

This book is not intended to be a complete guide. It is a pocket reference for those who don't want to spend $50 for a complete set of guides but do want to spend a week climbing in Vegas. This book covers a wide range of climbs at Red Rocks and Charleston. It includes gear routes, sport routes and multi-pitch routes at both areas.

As for amenities, Vegas is filled with buffets, hotels, motels, liquor stores and gas stations. The most convenient place to food shop when visiting Red Rocks is at Lucky's on Charleston and Rainbow (6 or 7 miles east of Red Rocks). For climbing/camping gear visit Desert Rock Sports (on Charleston Boulevard located about a block west of Rainbow). A new camping area, 13 Mile Campground, has been established just before you the Red Rocks Scenic Loop Road. The fee is a steep $10/night but includes picnic tables, toilets and water spigots—and it is the only legit' place to crash.

4   *Introduction*

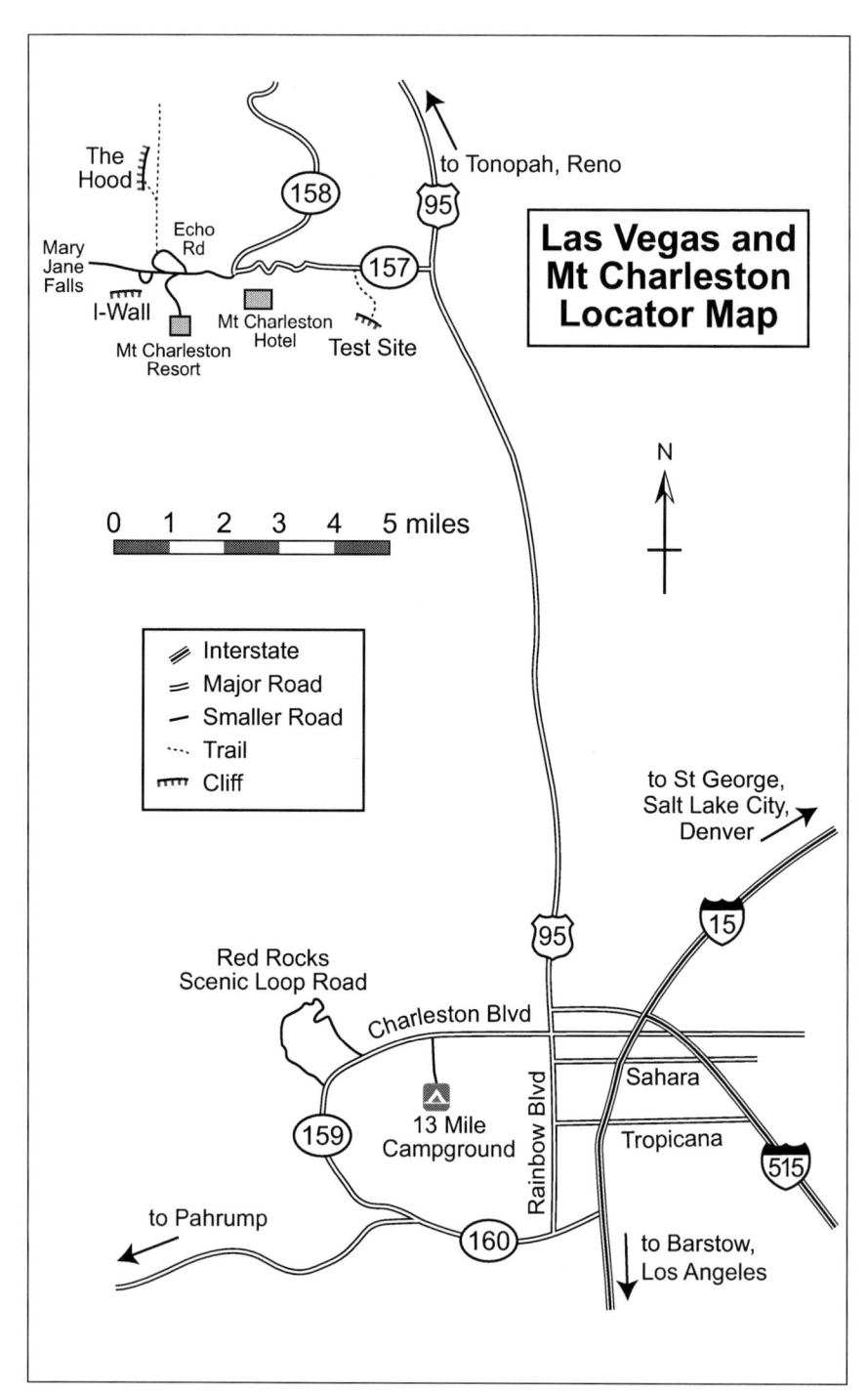

TABLE OF CONTENTS

MT. CHARLESTON AREA — 8
The Test Site — 9
Imagination Wall — 11
The Hood — 14
Infectious Cave — 15
Walk By Slab — 18
Corrosion Cave — 20
Cop Killer Cave — 21
South Central Slabs — 23
Wailing Souls Cave — 26
The Compton Cave — 28

RED ROCKS — 32
FIRST PULLOUT — 34
The Dog Wall — 34
The Fixx Cliff — 36
The Panty Wall — 37

SECOND PULLOUT — 39
The Tsunami Wall — 39
The Gallery — 41
The Wall of Confusion — 45

THIRD PULLOUT — 46
Sonic Youth Wall — 47
The Wake Up Wall — 49
The Sattelite — 51
The Trophy — 52

WILLOW SPRINGS AREA — 54
Ragged Edges — 54
Lost Creek Canyon/Left Out — 55
Icebox Canyon/Tarantula Wall — 57

BLACK VELVET CANYON — 58
Frogland Buttress — 58
Ixtalan Buttress — 59
Black Velvet Wall — 61

INDEX — 66

Sharp End Publishing
Authentic Guides From Core Climbers

Indian Creek:
A Climbing Guide
by David Bloom

WWW.SHARPENDBOOKS.COM
44 Titles and growing. Check us out!
1-888-594-6398

Mt. Charleston

Liv Sansov on on Soul Tran   photo: Jorge Visser

MT CHARLESTON AREA

Charleston is a climber's dream come true. Located approximately 45 minutes from downtown Vegas, it is easily reached by taking Hwy 95 north to Hwy 157 and then heading west. Obvious signs lead the way to Mt. Charleston making getting lost difficult. I've included The Hood, The Test Site and Imagination Wall because they are conveniently close to the camping area, easily accessed and offer a wide range of climbing. Mt. Charleston is situated in a high-alpine environment at about 8,000 feet, so be prepared for winter conditions including snow and frigid cold. This elevation also makes it an ideal summer crag.

Take Hwy 157 twenty miles west up towards Mt. Charleston. A fire station will be on your right at 19 miles and at 20 miles (where the road makes a sharp left turn) continue straight onto Echo Road. Echo Road quickly forks at a utility tank. Stay left and then make your first left into a dirt parking lot and camping area. Other camping areas are scattered throughout the Charleston area as it is mostly Forest Service land.

THE TEST SITE

Take Hwy 157 for 7.7 miles west until you reach a 55-mph sign. Turn left on the first dirt road immediately after this sign. Follow the 4WD road down into the dirt wash and follow it downstream. Continue down the wash through a tight bottleneck and park at 9.3 miles (from intersection of Highways 157 and 95). Hike up the adjoining wash about 20 minutes to a steep, well-marked and well-traveled trail on your left. Follow this trail up to the base of the cliff.

1. Self-Destruct Sequence 5.12a
Don't blow up as you follow the line of bolts just left of the seam.

2. Ground Zero 5.12c/d
Clip the first couple of bolts on Self-Destruct and then cut right.

3. Contamination 5.12a
Follow good steep ledges to the anchor of Ground Zero without getting' any of that stuff on your hands.

4. Glowing For It 5.10d
Stem your way up the steep dihedral.

5. Unknown 5.13a?
Follow the six bolts up through the pod and arching right.

6. Ashes To Ashes 5.13a
Climb the beautiful pockets and then the seam.

7. Countdown To Armageddon 5.13c
Time's ticking down on these small pockets and edges.

8. Unknown 5.13+?
Start in the perfect pockets right of Countdown and crank your way up to the thin crux.

9. Quark Corner 5.11b
Start on the gray slab right of the dihedral and then cut back left into the corner and up and left.

10. Ed's Route 5.12a
Ed must have some good crimper strength. Climb the vertical boulder past two bolts.

IMAGINATION WALL AND THE HOOD

Follow directions for Mt. Charleston on the previous page. At the utility tank turn right for The Hood or go straight and make your first left into a parking lot for Imagination Wall.

10   Mt. Charleston

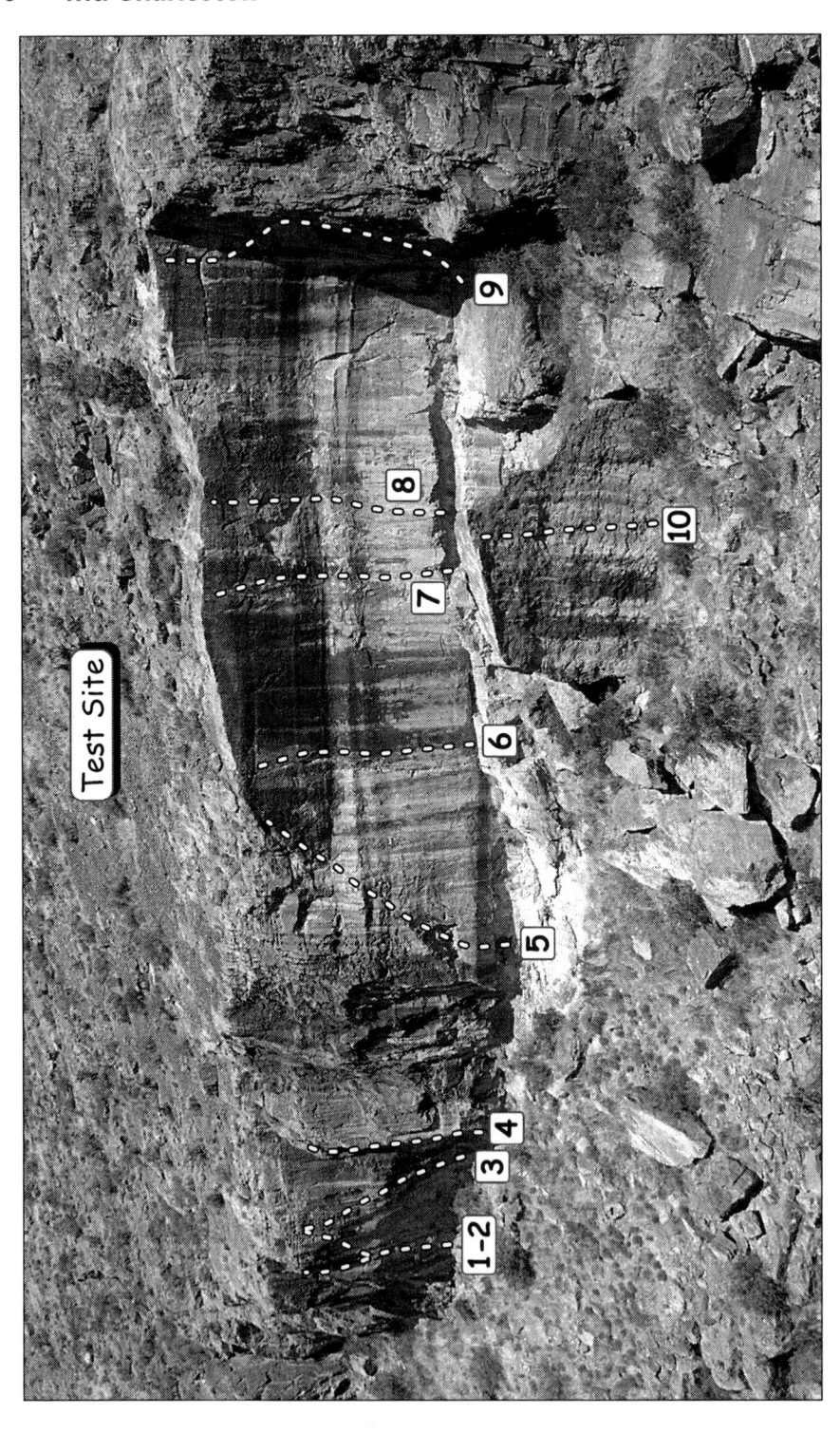

IMAGINATION WALL

This is the prominent blue and gray wall overlooking the parking lot. To approach this wall hike up the trail that follows the old rope-tow poles heading south from the east end of the parking lot. Follow this trail until it crests the top of the hill and then head west up the wash until close to the end of the wall. The trail will bring you to I-Wall Right.

Imagination Wall is divided into two parts; I-Wall Right and I-Wall Central Slabs. Routes are listed from right to left. Currently only one route ascends the entire wall (The three-pitch Imaginator) but people are working more routes to the top. There are about 20 one-pitch routes, with fun climbing on solution pockets and small edges.

Imagination Wall

I-Wall Right
1. Old World Order 5.11d
Climb the rightmost route past gold hangers. It has an old-world lack of steepness.
2. Civilized Fool 5.11b
Five feet left of Old World is a tan dihedral protected by more gold bolts.
3. Disconnect 5.10d
Jam up the wildly disconnected corner, through the rough then up and left.
4. Unknown 5.10+
Angle up the trough to the dicey gray slab.
5. Unknown 5.10+
Same start but head left up the easier slab.
6. Almost Real 5.6
Almost real climbing up the enormous gray slab to rap-rings.

I-Wall Central Slabs
7. Repaginator 5.10+?
Grunge yourself past five bolts and vegetation to triangular slings 60 feet right of Imaginator.
8. Imaginator 5.11c, 5.11a, 5.11a
Navigate your way up these three long pitches.
9. Unknown 5.11
Start ten feet left of Imaginator, bust the small roof and slab your way up to chains.
10. Collective Peace 5.12a
Dude, be cool when you're crimping up the ripples through a small roof.
11. Selective War 5.11a
Five feet left of Collective Peace is a line of seven bolts that heads up and left of the tan roof.
12. Honest Politician 5.11c
Yeah right! Clip three bolts and head right to the anchors of Selective War.
13. Fighting For Peace 5.11c
Start as for Honest, but climb straight up to the top of the pillar.
14. Perfect World 5.12a
Start ten feet left of Fighting For Peace, clip three bolts and join Fighting For Peace.
15. Flying Pig 5.10c
Clip six bolts on mottled gray stone up to the top of the pillar.

Imagination Wall 13

Imagination Wall - Center

16. Unknown 5.11c
Climb past eight bolts just right of a small overhanging, left-facing dihedral.
17. Exacto Blade 5.11d
Begin 20 feet left of #16, go up and over the lip.
18. Unknown 5.10c
Follow good edges and sidepulls up to the start of the white rock.
19. Unknown 5.11c
Send the dicey gray bulge 20 feet left of #18. Be careful clipping the second bolt; it's way up there,

THE HOOD

The Hood is one of the sickest sport climbing areas in America with a plethora of routes on severely overhanging, polished and pocketed limestone. Most of the routes are in the 5.12-5.13 range but there are a handful of easier warm-ups in the 5.10 and 5.11 range. Situated at nearly 8,000 feet, The Hood faces south and gets plenty of sun making it a little too hot to climb during the middle of the day during the summer, but ideal for winter, spring and fall.

To reach The Hood continue up Echo Road about an eighth of a mile past the fork at the utility shed and park at the North Loop Trail trailhead on your left. Hike about ten minutes up this trail until you get your first view of Infectious Cave and cross the wash on the well-worn trail and head up the steep trail to Corrosion Cave.

THE HOOD OVERVIEW
1. Corrosion Cave
2. Cop Killa Cave
3. Wailing Souls Cave
4. The Compton Cave
5. Infectious Cave
6. South Central Slabs

INFECTIOUS CAVE
This is the furthest-left cave at The Hood.
1. Unknown 5.9
A totally schwaggy warm-up on the far left wall just past Infectious Cave.
2. Doo Doo Love 5.9
Similar to #1.
3. Charleston 5.10b
Another short warm-up just left of Slaughterhouse.
4. Slaughterhouse 5.12b
A short but hard route past four bolts on small edges and pockets.
5. Gorillas In The Mist 5.12d
Follow the bolts up and right just left of the cave and behind a large pine tree.
6. Ghetto Boyz 5.13c
Start in the middle of the cave on jugs and then head left through slopers and pockets to cold-shuts. Clip the fifh bolt on your left and head left.
7. Ghetto Booty 5.14b
Climb Ghetto Boyz but go straight up at the sixth bolt past seven more bolts.

Infectious Groove

8. Infectious Groove 5.13b
Start the same as for Ghetto Boyz but climb straight up the groove to the anchor.
9. Infectious Booty 5.14b
Cut left through the black roof from #8's last bolt, and finish on #7's anchors.
10. Molotov Cocktail 5.13a
Start ten feet right of Infectious, and 15 feet off the ground, and climb past seven bolts to the Infectious anchor.
11. Urban Decay 5.12c/d
Start on the detached slab five feet right of #10 and climb past small edges to the Infectious anchor.

There are two bolted slab climbs to the right of the cave that go at 5.6 and 5.7.

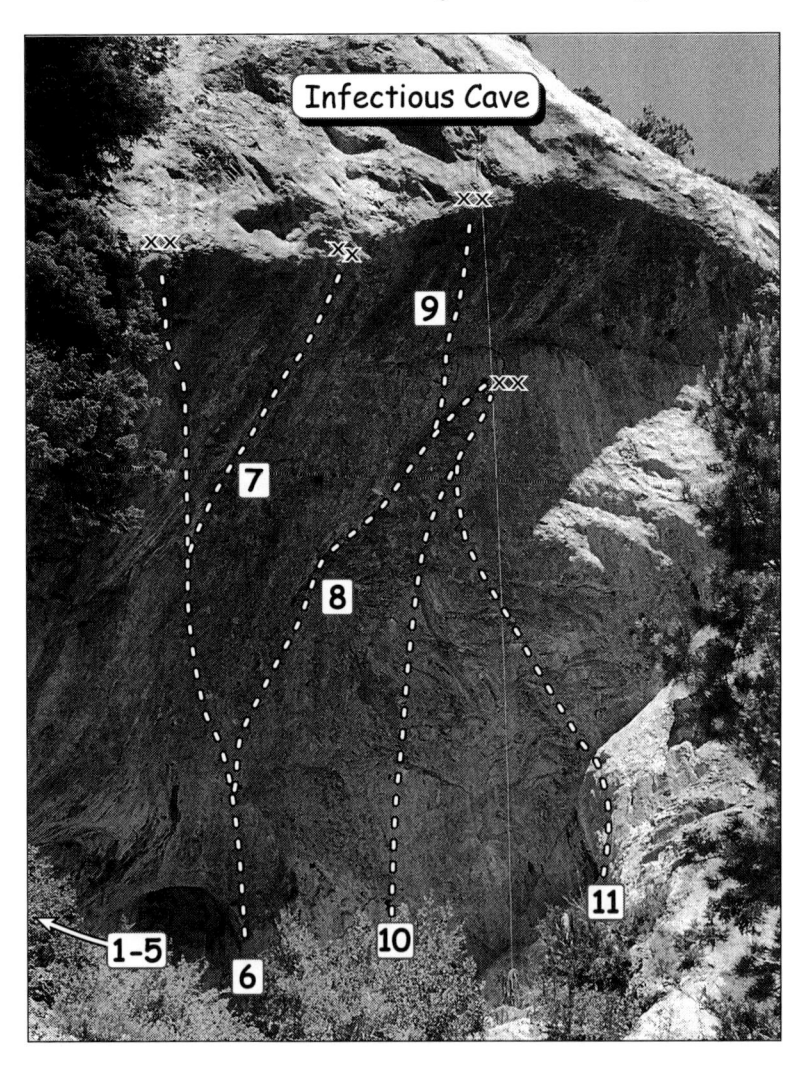

The Hood 17

The author on Urban Decay   photo: John Dunn

Walk By Slab

This is the slab directly left of Corrosion Cave. This slab is host to some great warm-ups in the 5.10-5.11 range. None of the routes are named except the last one closest to Corrosion Cave.

1. 5.11b
Climb the furthest-left route up the brownish-gray streak past seven bolts.

2. 5.11a
Begin five feet right, clip two bolts and then cut left to meet up with #1.

3. 5.11c
Same start but continue straight up past six bolts to anchors.

4. 5.11b
Same start but after the third bolt take the right variation past two bolts and then cut back left to rejoin #3.

5. 5.11c
Begin about 20 feet right of last route about 20 feet up some broken ledges. Follow the line of six bolts angling left to meet up with the anchors of #3.

6. 5.12a
Climb the right side of the orange corner, about ten feet right of #5, heading up and left to hidden anchors under an overhang.

7. 5.12c
Same start as for #6 but at the seventh bolt cut up and right over a steep bulge aiming for the anchors up and right of the last set of anchors.

8. 5.12a
Start 20 feet right and below #6 just left of Corrosion Cave. Climb past seven bolts up to the anchors in the Y-notch; continue past the left-angling seam to the anchors of #6.

9. 5.12c
Same route as #8 but head up and right after clipping the 12th bolt.

10. 5.10a
Begin the same as for #8 and #9 but stop at the first set of anchors.

11. 5.10d
Same start as #10 but cut out right after the fifth bolt heading to the same anchors as #10.

12. 5.12d
Climb up to the set of anchors in the Y-notch and continue up and right clipping four more bolts and then taking the left line clipping one more bolt and then the anchors. Thirteen bolts in all.

13. 5.12c
Same route as #12 but take the right line near the top heading up and right through the right-facing corner to the anchors. Fourteen bolts.

14. Friendly Fire 1 5.11d
Share the start as the last routes but head right after clipping the fourth bolt, eventually hooking up with Warlords.

The Hood 19

15. Friendly Fire 2 5.13a
Climb past the anchors of Warlords clipping another ten bolts, cranking through a steep roof and finally clipping another set of anchors near the top of the wall.

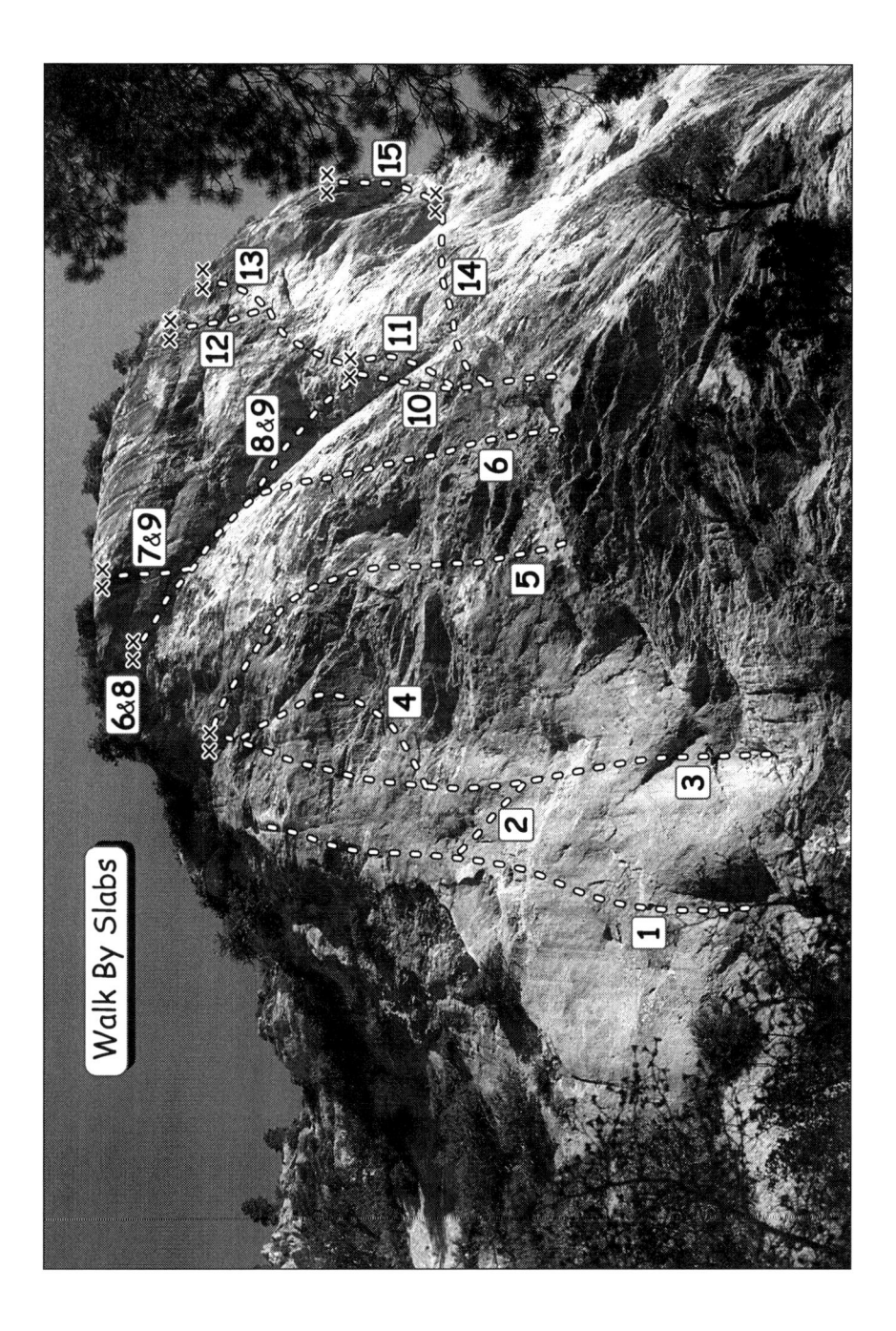

CORROSION CAVE

This is the first cave you come to when you hike up to The Hood. It is ornately decorated with seeping cracks and enormous solution pockets.

1. Short But Stout 5.12c
Like a warm shot of stiff whiskey!! Climb the first three bolts of Screaming Target then cut left out the low lip of the cave.

2. Warlord 5.13a
Start on the rad jug-haul of Screaming Target, climb past four bolts and then cut left around the lip past four more bolts.

3. Screaming Target 5.13c
Traverse right along the left lip of the cave past seven bolts.

4. Corrosion 5.13a
Ascend the amazing solution pockets in the middle of the cave straight up to the anchor.

5. Corrosion Extension 5.13b
From the anchors of Corrosion continue straight up to a second anchor.

6. Across The Universe 5.11c
Start on the far right side of the cave and navigate your way up and left through amazing pockets to the anchors of Corrosion.

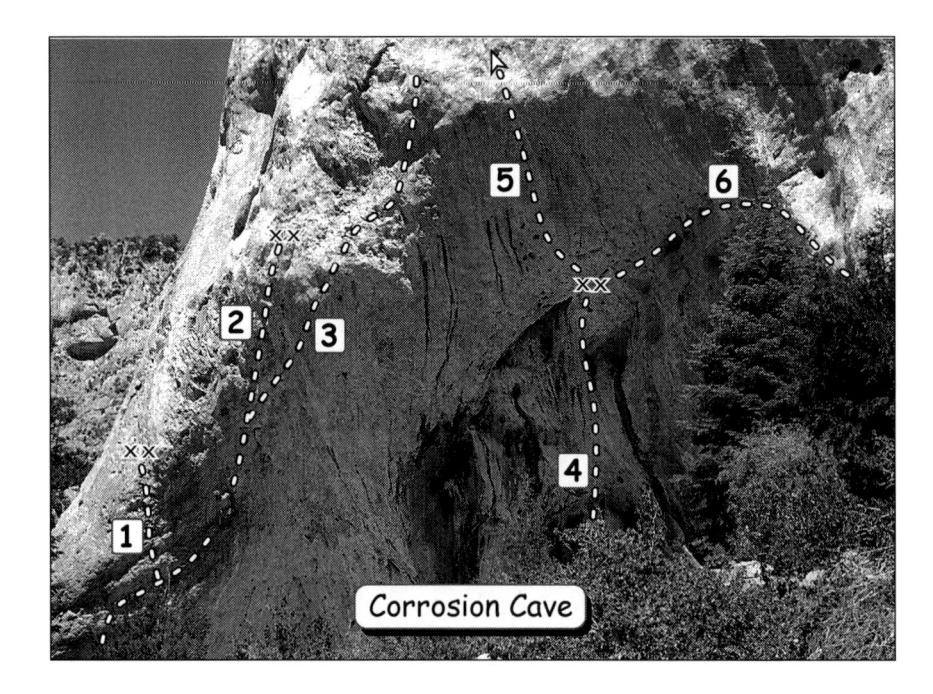

Corrosion Cave

COP KILLER CAVE
This is the next cave, 20 feet right of Across The Universe, that one must scramble 15 feet up a slab to access.

1. Malt Liquor Man 5.11a, 5.11c
The leftmost route in this cave is a two-pitch slab climb that climbs up and left on the large slab above and right of Across The Universe.

2. Gun Tower 1 5.12a
Start at the left lip of the cave and head straight up.

3. Gun Tower 2 5.12c
Same start as for Gun Tower but continue straight up past the anchors into a polished face.

4. Gun Tower 3
At the anchor head right past three extra bolts.

5. Bloodbath 1 5.12d
Climb the shallow pockets directly right of #2, angling up and right through some wicked-cool pockets under the roof and then bust up to the Cop Killer anchors.

6. Bloodbath 2 5.12d
Follow the same line but instead of heading up to the anchor continue up and right to the anchors for Heatin' Up The Hood.

7. Ricochet 5.12d
Start 20 feet right of #5, climb through the bulge then angle right under the lip through pockets to end at Cop Killer anchors.

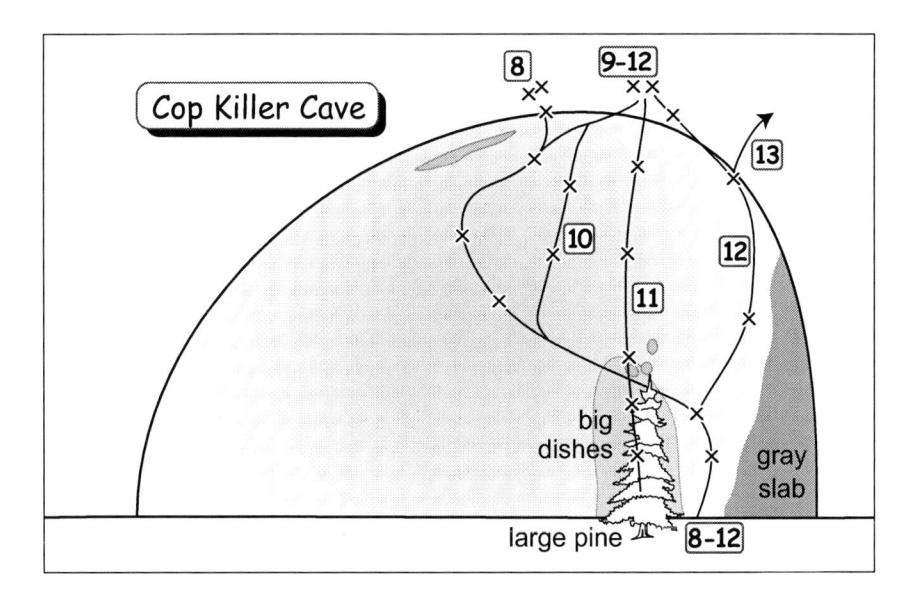

8. Cop Killer 5.12a
Load your weapon in the far right side of the scoop behind the pine tree, clip two bolts heading into the obvious huge second hueco and make your way to the anchors up and left. There are two bolts, five feet left, which can be used as a variation to this and the next four routes.

9. Heatin' Up The Hood 1 5.11c
Start as for Cop Killer and traverse left to the obvious hole under the lip on Ricochet. From here traverse back hard right to the anchors above the start of the route.

10. Heatin' Up The Hood 2 5.11d
Use the same start but don't go all the way over to the hole on Ricochet. Instead take the bolts that are just left of the obvious hueco.

11. Heatin' Up The Hood 3 5.12a
The thin pockets above the two huecos might just toast your tips! Same start as for #10 but after the second bolt climb left and then straight up through the two obvious huecos.

12. Witness To A Killin' 1 5.11b
You ain't seen nothin' yet. Begin as for #11 and head straight up the slabby shoulder, heading out and right onto the face after the second bolt. Clip two more bolts and then cut back left to the anchors of #11.

13. Witness To A Killin' 2 5.10d
Same start as for #12 but keep heading right on the face.

14. Witness To A Killin' 3 5.12b
A two-bolt extension of the previous route using tiny pockets in the gray face above.

15. Witness To A Killin' 4 5.12c
Continue past the last anchor and clip the next anchor up and right of the pod.

16. Witness This! 5.13b
This route will put you in a witness relocation program somewhere near the top of the cliff. Bust the roof above the anchors heading right and then swerve back left up the slab towards the top of the cliff. 18 bolts!!

SOUTH CENTRAL SLABS

These slabs are directly right of the Cop Killer cave and include a good number of awesome 5.12 pocketed climbs on beautiful water-streaked slabs.

17. Blue Man 5.6
Super slab climb for someone who may be blue. Twenty feet right and below the start of Witness.

18. Grandma Beth 5.10d
Granny must be bold putting only two bolts in this 5.10d. The route above is a super-hard extension; grade unknown.

19. Cut Your Hair Sister 5.10d
Begin trimming ten feet right of #18, clip four bolts angling up and right.

20. Toprope 5.12a
Toprope the route directly below the anchors of #19.

21. Wired 1 5.12c
Better have two shots of espresso for this one. Climb the left-arching line of 12 bolts up the smooth face and finishing on a super-cool pocketed seam heading directly left.

22. Wired 2 5.12c
On second thoughts—make it a Mocha Grande. Begin with same start as #21 but at sixth bolt climb up and right and then back left to the anchor.

23. Wired 3 5.12c
Oh what the hell, just throw in some speed too! Climb up like #22 but continue up and right at the 11th bolt past three more bolts to the anchors of Boyz In The Hood.

24. Rappin' Boyz 1 5.12a
Vanilla Ice and Eminem ain't got nothin' on this route. It's kinda neat, you oughta freak. Climb the black water streak, 15 feet right of #23, angling up and left to a two-bolt anchor.

25. Mo Betta 5.12b
Continue left past the anchors of Rappin' Boyz and hook up with the anchors of Wired 2.

26. Rappin' Boyz 2 5.12c
From the first set of anchors, pull on crankers, straight up to the anchors of Wired 3.

27. Boyz In The Hood 5.12c
Grab your Glocks and unload the clip! Climb the first four bolts of Rappin' Boyz and then climb straight up eventually angling left to the anchors.

28. Jazz Ma Tazz 1 5.12c
Kick it in 4/4, key of C. Fifteen feet right of Rappin' Boyz is a shallow groove with vegetation. Begin here and crimp your way past seven bolts.

29. Jazz Ma Tazz 2 5.13b
Climb out the right side of the roof above the anchors up the steep headwall to reach an enormous slab.

30. The Dark Side 5.12c
Luke, embrace the crimpers 15 feet right of the last route.
31. Endless Needs And Bloody Deeds 5.12c
Ascend to the second bolt of Dark Side and cut out right and follow the eight bolts to the anchors.

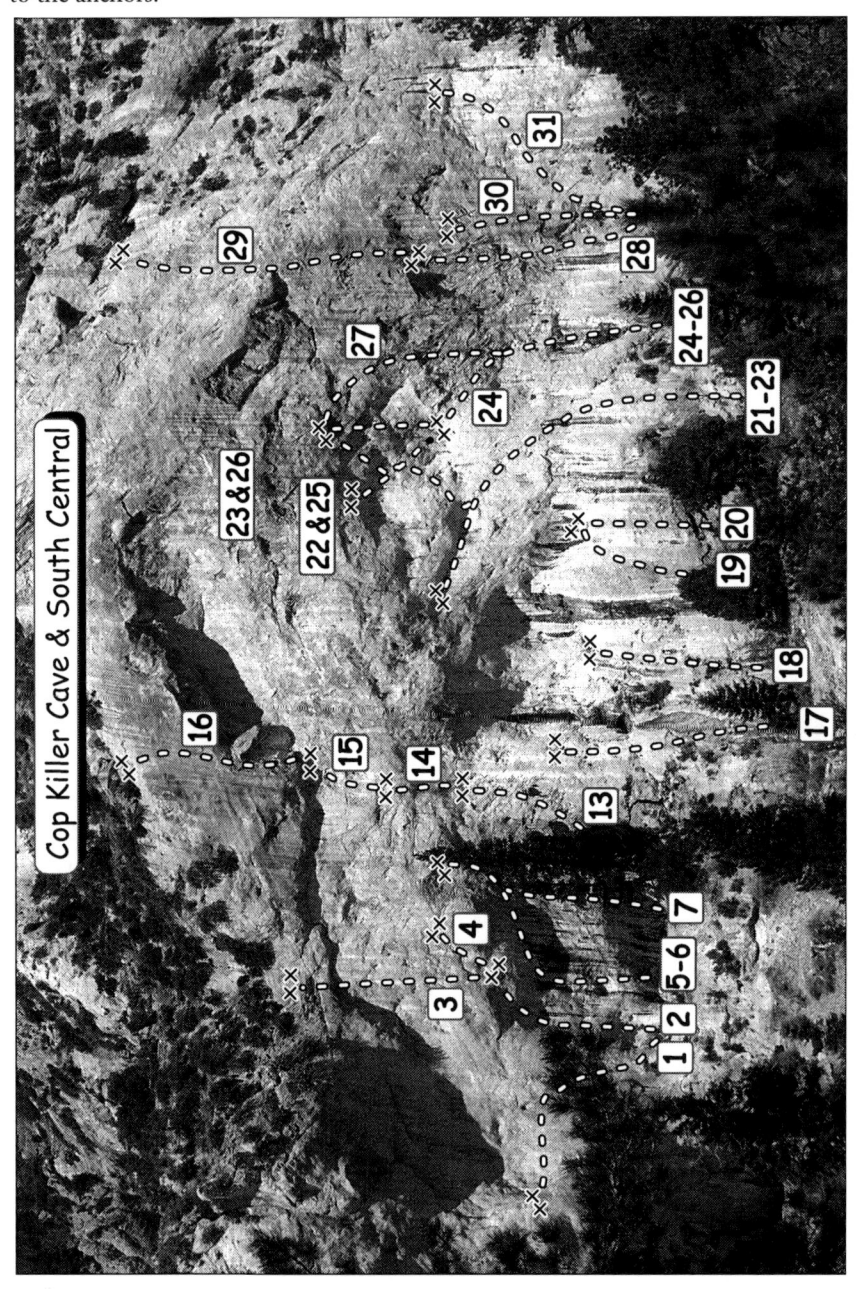

John Dunn on Ghetto Boys

WAILING SOULS CAVE
This is the small, ultra-steep cave between South Central and the Compton Cave. This cave is riddled with contrived lines linking multiple routes to make up new routes.

1. Bloodline 1 5.12b
On the beautiful blue wall directly left of the cave proper are two magnificent climbs. Bloodline is the leftmost route here and climbs up and left of a giant pod on awesome pockets.

2. Bloodline 2 5.12c
Head right after clipping the first bolt and finish on Borderline.

3. Borderline 5.13a
This is directly right of Bloodline and climbs through pockets and slopers to the anchors of Bloodline.

4. Run For The Border 5.13b
Clip the first couple of bolts on Borderline and grab yourself a taco at the next set of anchors up and right.

5. Run For The Border Extension 5.13d
Make the Chihuahua proud and finish on the anchors for Wailing Souls.

6. Hyper Soul 5.14a
Start on the far left side of the cave and climb up to the anchors of Wailing Souls.

7. Primal Soul 5.14a
Start in the deepest part of the cave, ten feet right of Hyper Soul, and clip five bolts and the finish on Wailing Souls.

8. Wailing Souls 5.13d
Start on the far right side of the cave at a right-facing flake. Climb past five bolts angling left and finish up near the top of the blue streak above the left side of the cave.

9. Soul Man 5.13d
Begin as for Wailing Souls but at the seventh bolt cut up and right.

10. Soul Train 5.14a
Climb straight up the thin blue streak five feet right of Wailing Souls.

11. Project 5.?
Just right of Soul Train is a one-bolt project.

12. Hoodlum 5.12a
Climb the four bolts 25 feet right of Soul Train.

The Hood 27

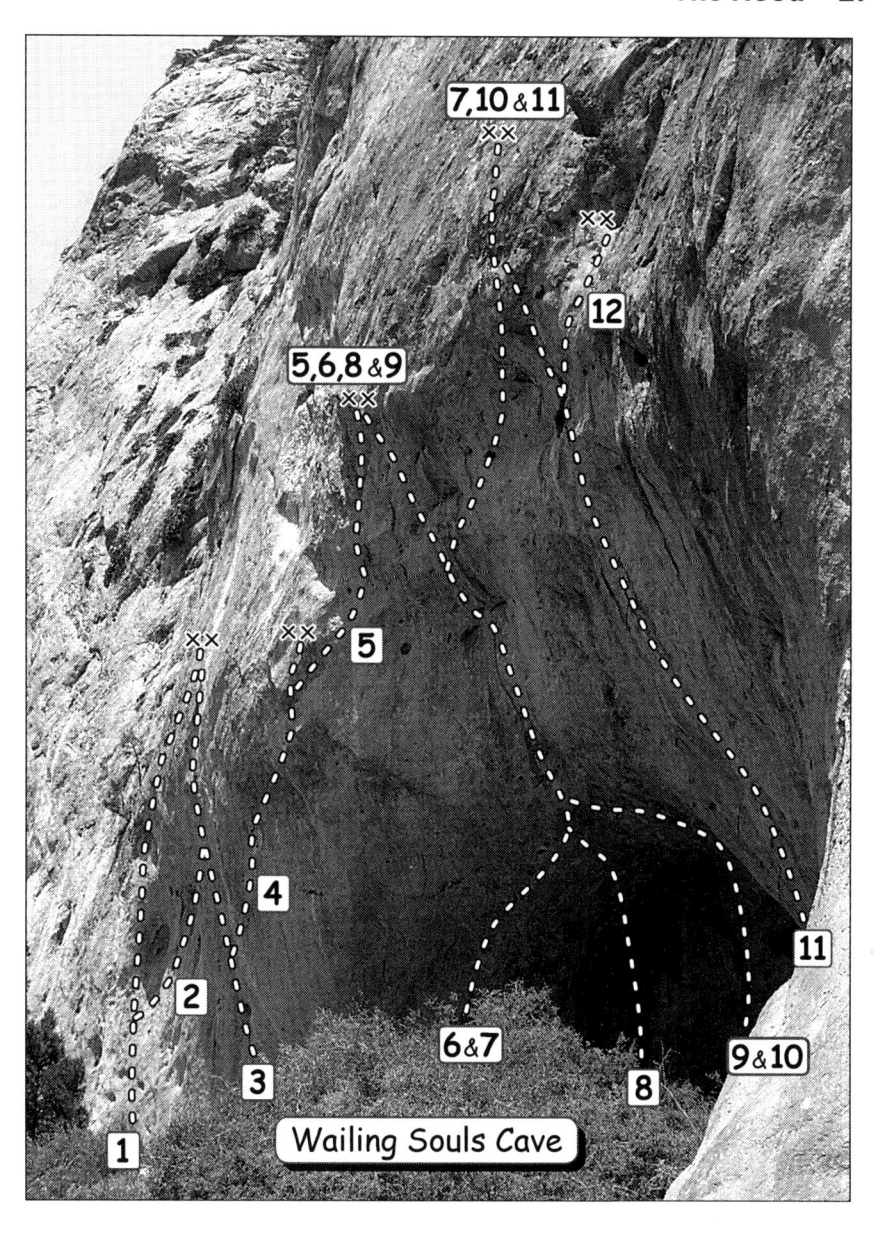

Wailing Souls Cave

THE COMPTON CAVE

This is the largest cave at The Hood and hosts some of the hardest and longest routes here. Just left of the cave proper are some slab climbs that range from 5.9 to 5.11c.

1. Equalizer 5.13a
The first route on the left side of the cave. Awesome route but tight quarters for the digits.

2. Closing Down 5.14a
Clip the seven bolts that make up the second route in from the lip of the cave.

3. Facile 5.14b
Climb the extension of Closing Down past three more bolts.

4. Hasta La Manana 5.14b/c
Clip the first four bolts of Closing Down and then head up and right past eight more bolts to the anchors.

5. Hasta La Vista 5.14b
Ascend Hasta La Manana and climb past the anchors up to a second set of anchors with three bolts.

6. Legend 5.14a
Start 20 feet right of Closing Down. Clip five bolts and then cut left to join Closing Down up to the first set of anchors.

7. Legend Of The Overfiend 5.14b
Climb past five bolts just right of Closing Down and then finish on Facile.

8. Free At Last 5.13d
Directly right of Legends is a ten-bolt line that climbs up past two large holes. Project 5.?

9. Straight Outa Compton 5.12d/13a
Located in the deepest part of the cave is a stellar route through big pods and a knee-bar rest.

10. Straight Outa Compton/Animal Attack 5.13b/c
Start on Straight Outa Compton and at the last bolt before the anchors cut out right and finish on Animal Attack, clipping five more bolts.

11 Animal Attack 5.12c
Begin fifteen feet right of Straight Outa Compton. Climb up to the left-angling seam and follow it to the anchors of Straight Outa Compton.

12 Animal Attack Extension 5.13b
Climb past the first five bolts of Animal Attack and then bust up and right over a pocketed bulge to the anchors.

13. Energizer 5.13a
Begin 20 feet right of Animal Attack and follow the left-angling line of nine bolts through pockets to Straight Outa Compton.
Projects 5.? These are the next two lines of bolts right of Energizer.

14. Shit Jaws 5.12b
Climb the rightmost line of bolts, just right of the main cave in a little sub-cave.

The Hood 29

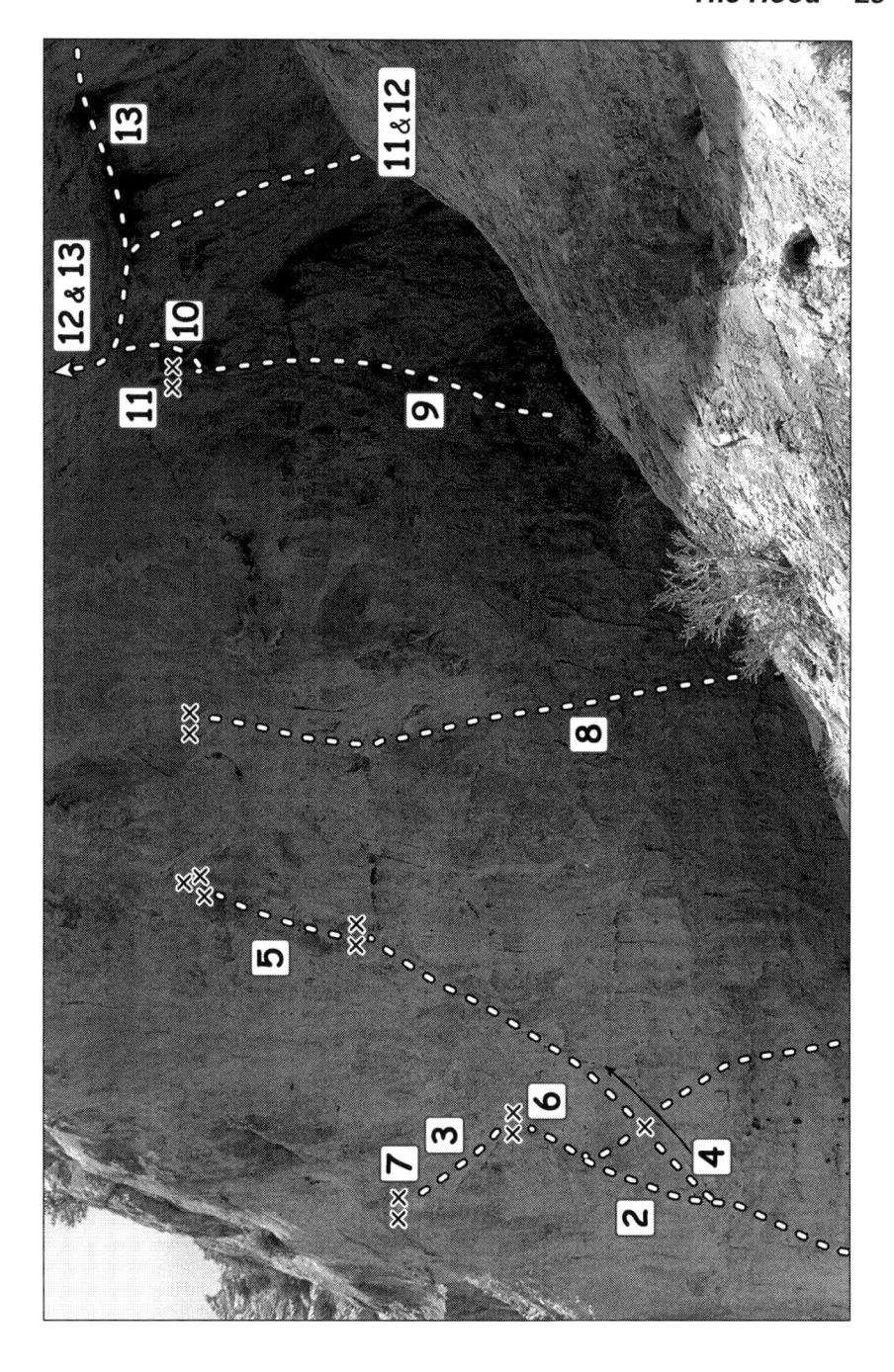

Mt. Charleston

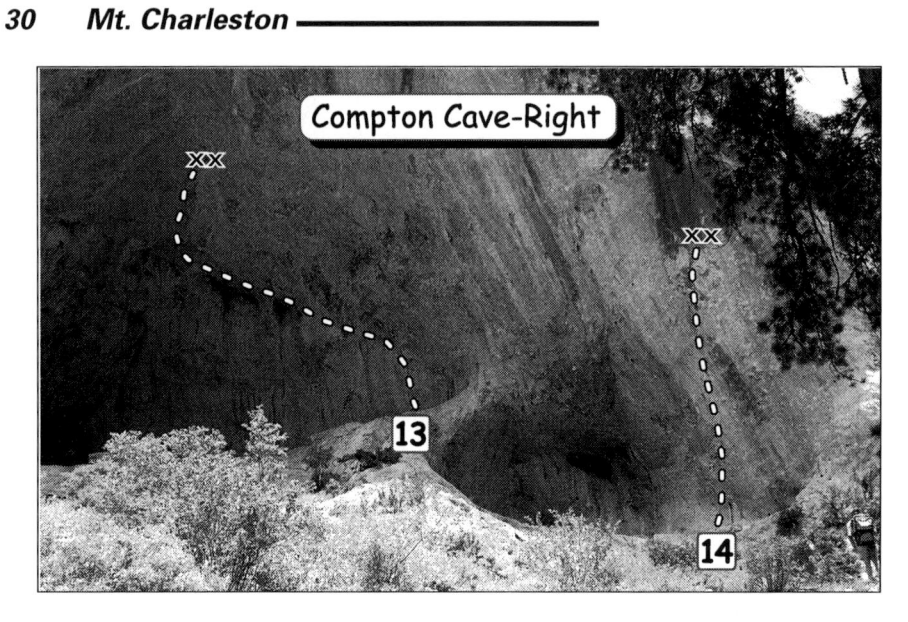

Compton Cave-Right

RED ROCKS

Fred Knapp on Mistral in the Gallery   photo: Sharon Powers

RED ROCKS

With almost 1000 routes on hard varnished sandstone, usually littered with holds, Red Rocks provides an opportunity for years of exploration. The rock here offers crimpers, jugs and slopers more readily than some of the ladies walking the streets offer their goods. Most of the climbs are well bolted (not all of them) but many gear routes await the adventurous.

Red Rocks is the ideal winter cragging area. When temps reach freezing points around the country, Red Rocks is usually a balmy 65-70 degrees. Also, during the sweltering summer months when temps in Vegas reach into the hundreds, some of the shady walls are well within the comfort zone for climbing. One just has to be selective when choosing a crag to hang at.

The crags here are listed in the order they are reached by following the one-way loop road. Crags reached from the first pullout are listed first; crags accessed by the second pullout are listed next; and so on. Climbs are listed from left to right unless otherwise mentioned.

To reach Red Rocks, take Charleston Blvd. west out of town (about 15 miles) until you reach the BLM entrance station and scenic loop road. Turn right on this one-way road and the pleasures of Red Rocks will be at your fingertips. Note: The rangers report recent instances of break-ins of climber's cars along this road. The thieves have been stealing credit cards from wallets, but also carefully replacing them with similar-looking old ones, and re-locking the car, so they have more time to figure out exactly what your credit limit is. Don't leave your wallet in your car!

Index   33

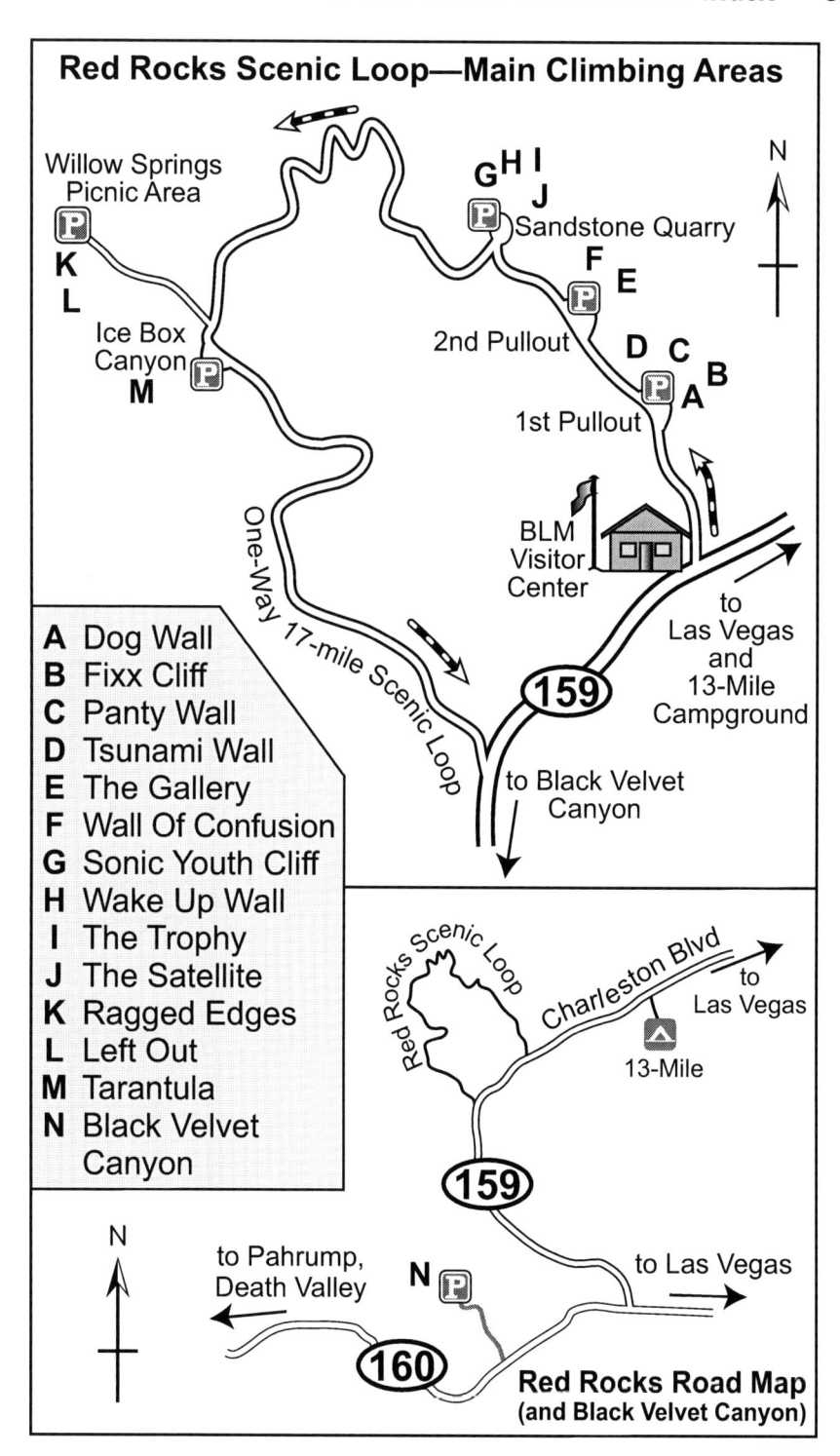

Red Rocks Scenic Loop—Main Climbing Areas

A Dog Wall
B Fixx Cliff
C Panty Wall
D Tsunami Wall
E The Gallery
F Wall Of Confusion
G Sonic Youth Cliff
H Wake Up Wall
I The Trophy
J The Satellite
K Ragged Edges
L Left Out
M Tarantula
N Black Velvet Canyon

Red Rocks Road Map
(and Black Velvet Canyon)

FIRST PULLOUT
(The Dog Wall, The Fixx Cliff and The Panty Wall)

The Dog Wall

The Dog Wall is reached by hiking down the observation trail then veering left on the well-worn trail into the large wash and then heading up and left in the wash about another 75 yards. From the parking lot, this cliff appears as the lowest good cliff.

1. Wok The Dog 5.7
Climb the leftmost right-leaning ramp.

2. Cat Walk 5.10a
About 40 feet right of Wok The Dog is a right-leaning ramp. Climb straight up to the first bolt (scary) or traverse in left from the ramp and climb past four bolts to the anchors.

3. It's A Bitch 5.10b
Start with a scary traverse five feet right of Catwalk and clip four bolts to the anchors.

4. Man's Best Friend 5.10
Climb the aforementioned right-leaning ramp and finish up the dicey, hard to protect face.
5. Here Kitty, Kitty 5.11c
Start 30 feet right of Man's Best Friend and climb the bulge past four bolts to the anchors on the slab.
6. K-9 5.12b
Climb through the left side of the pod five feet right of Here Kitty and finish up on small crimpers.
7. Cujo 5.11d
Follow the white streak past a hand-ledge up to the thin crux.
8. Poodle Chainsaw Massacre 5.11c
Climb way up the slab to the first bolt (20 feet) then head straight up through long reaches on small holds.

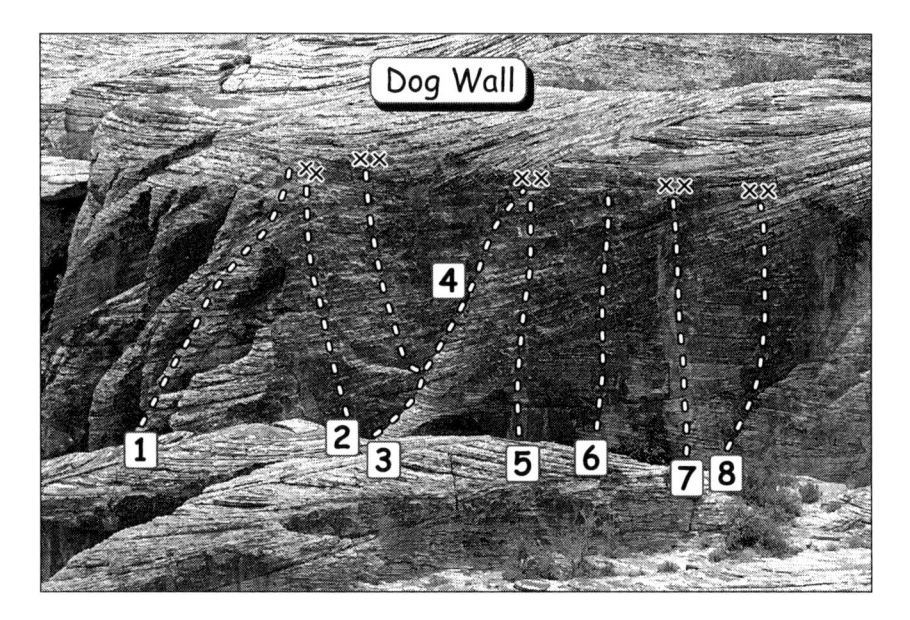

THE FIXX CLIFF
This cliff is located directly uphill from the Dog Wall and is a gear climbers delight. Unlike most crags at Red Rocks, this cliff is not bolt protected and requires diligent gear placement by the leader. Descend down the right side of the cliff.

1. The Whiff 5.10a
Follow the varnished hand/finger crack up the left side of the wall.
2. Snow Blind 5.11 R
Climb the vertical huecos past one bolt above a pod just right of The Whiff.
3. Stand Or Fall 5.11a
Climb past big pockets past a bolt into the black S-crack.
4. Crack 5.11b
Jam your way up the prominent left-facing crack ten feet right of Stand Or Fall
5. Free Base 5.11
Ten feet right of Crack is a crack that takes good gear and then follows an overhanging seam past three bolts.
6. Saved By Zero 5.11
Stuff your fingers into the obvious black crack ten feet right of Free Base.
7. Red Skies 5.11d
Start ten feet right of Saved By Zero in a thin seam with less than desirable gear and crank your way up past three more bolts.

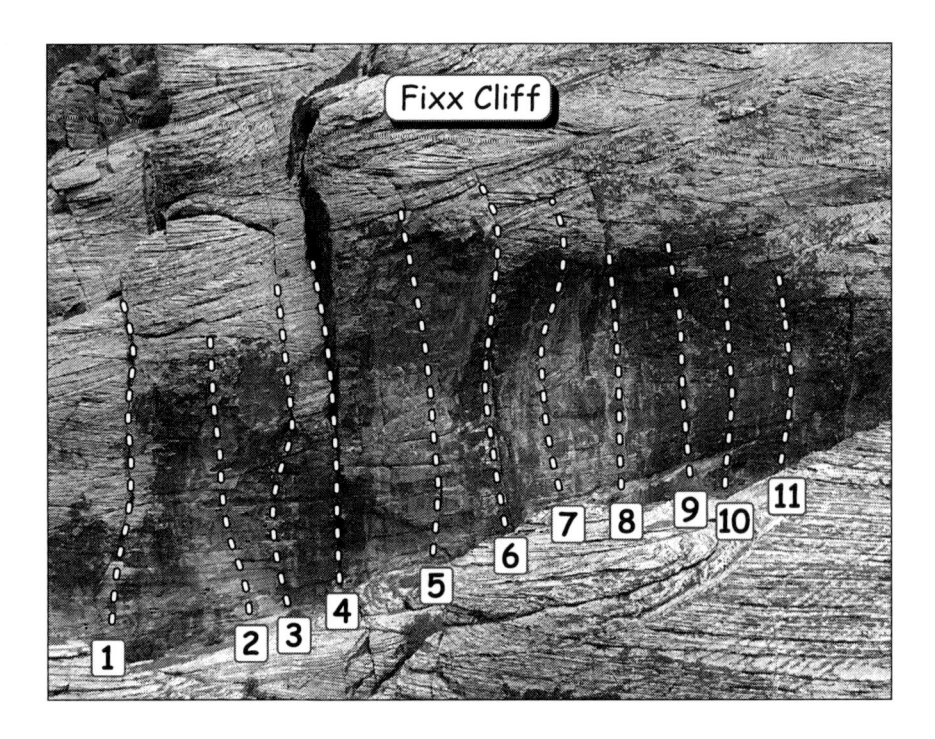

8. The Geezer 5.11b
Climb the pink face just right of Red Skies past a drilled piton up into the white crack. Once again, dicey gear below the piton will have you pondering "Why am I here?"

9. Cocaine Hotline 5.11
Climb the thin black crack past tiny gear then past one bolt.

10. Reach The Beach 5.11
Six feet right of Cocaine Hotline is a small boulder. Climb the seam utilizing better gear placements and pass one bolt.

11. Eight Ball 5.11
This is the last seam that has a bolt protecting it on the right side of the wall.

There are five more thin seams to the right that get shorter as you head right. Don't even bother.

THE PANTY WALL
This is the obvious black cliff that sits up high and left when viewed from the first pullout. To reach the cliff hike down the observation trail but don't go down into the wash, instead follow the obvious trail left towards the second pullout over a small knoll. Continue down this trail until you hit a wash and then cut right to gain some slabs on the backside of a massive piece of red rock and hike up to the cliff. You'll be approaching this cliff from the southwest.

1. Totally Clips 5.11+
On the steeper left side of the wall, this is the leftmost route, past six bolts to a chain anchor.

2. Unknown 5.12a
Just right of Totally Clips is another bolt-route with eight bolts past small edges leading up to an anchor.

3. Unknown 5.10+
Just left of the prominent arete that separates the two sides of the wall is a bolt line with six bolts and anchors. Clip the first five bolts on the left side of the arete, turn a lip, head right and clip the last bolt to gain the anchors.

4. Edible Panties 5.10+
Ascend the right-leaning crack at the bottom of the arete and bust up the blocky wall to the anchors located in a V-shaped notch.

5. Panty Raid 5.10
Start 35 feet right of Edible Panties behind the large pine tree. Make your way up to the varnished section of the wall and follow a right-angling crack to the anchors over the lip.

6. Panty Line 5.10a
Begin ten feet right of Panty Raid just behind the rightmost boulder at the base of the cliff. Climb the right side of the varnished wall up to the anchor located over the lip (above where it looks like a piece of varnish broke off).

7. Unknown 5.10a
Begin 30 feet up the ramp right of Panty Line and follow the line of seven bolts that starts under a shallow roof.

8. Silk Panties 5.7
Follow the five-bolt line right of #7.

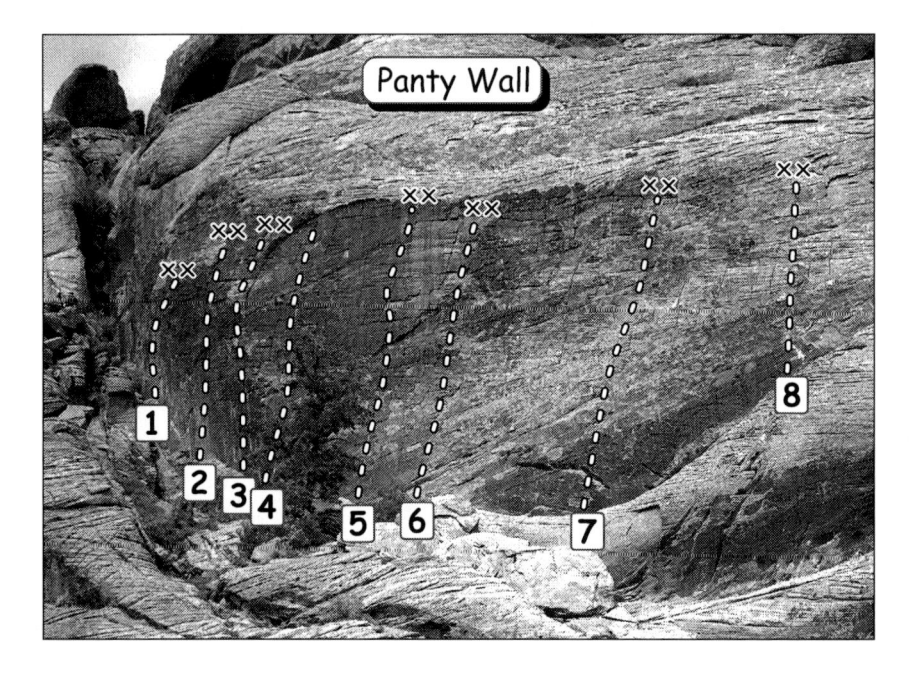

SECOND PULLOUT
(TSUNAMI WALL, THE GALLERY and THE WALL OF CONFUSION)

The Tsunami Wall
This wall is situated between the two parking areas and is recognized by its overhanging wave-like shape. Approach from either parking area. To reach it from the first pullout hike as if going to the Panty Wall but instead of cutting up and right to the Panty Wall, continue on the trail towards the second pullout on the well-traveled trail. To reach it from the second pullout, hike back along the road towards the first pullout until perpendicular with said wall. From here, follow the trail that heads towards the wall, skirting right around the obvious red outcroppings and straight up to the crag.

1. Poseidon Adventure 5.12b
This is on the very left side of the Tsunami Wall proper. Power your way past four bolts to open-shuts around the left side of a concavity on the steep block.

2. Barracuda 5.13b
Crank up the leftmost bolt route on the Tsunami Wall proper.

3. Land Shark 5.12b
Rope up ten feet right of Barracuda behind a large detached block and climb up and left past six bolts.

4. The Angler 5.12c
Clip the first three bolts of Land Shark and then go straight up after the third bolt past four more bolts.

5. Threadfin 5.12c
Start as per The Angler but follow the rightmost line of bolts to an anchor at the lip.

6. SOS 5.13a
Ten feet right of the start of Land Shark is another large block at the bottom of the wall. Start on the left side of this block, cruise up and left to a horn then follow a thin seam to the top.

7. Man Overboard! 5.12d
Start five feet right of SOS, on the same block, and follow the line of bolts—without falling over.

8. Aftershock 5.12b
Begin off the right side of the block and crimp your way past five bolts.

9. Abandon Ship 5.12a
Climb the rightmost bolt line (angling up and left from the bottom of the dihedral) at the right side of the Tsunami Wall proper.

10. Women And Children First 5.7
Jam your way up the dihedral that separates the "Wave" from the right block. This is the only route on this wall that is less than vertical.

40   Red Rocks

11. Tremor 5.10
Climb the first bolt route right of Women And Children.
12. Low Tide 5.10
Follow the bolt line ten feet right of Tremor. Tremor and Low Tide are good warm-ups for the other routes.

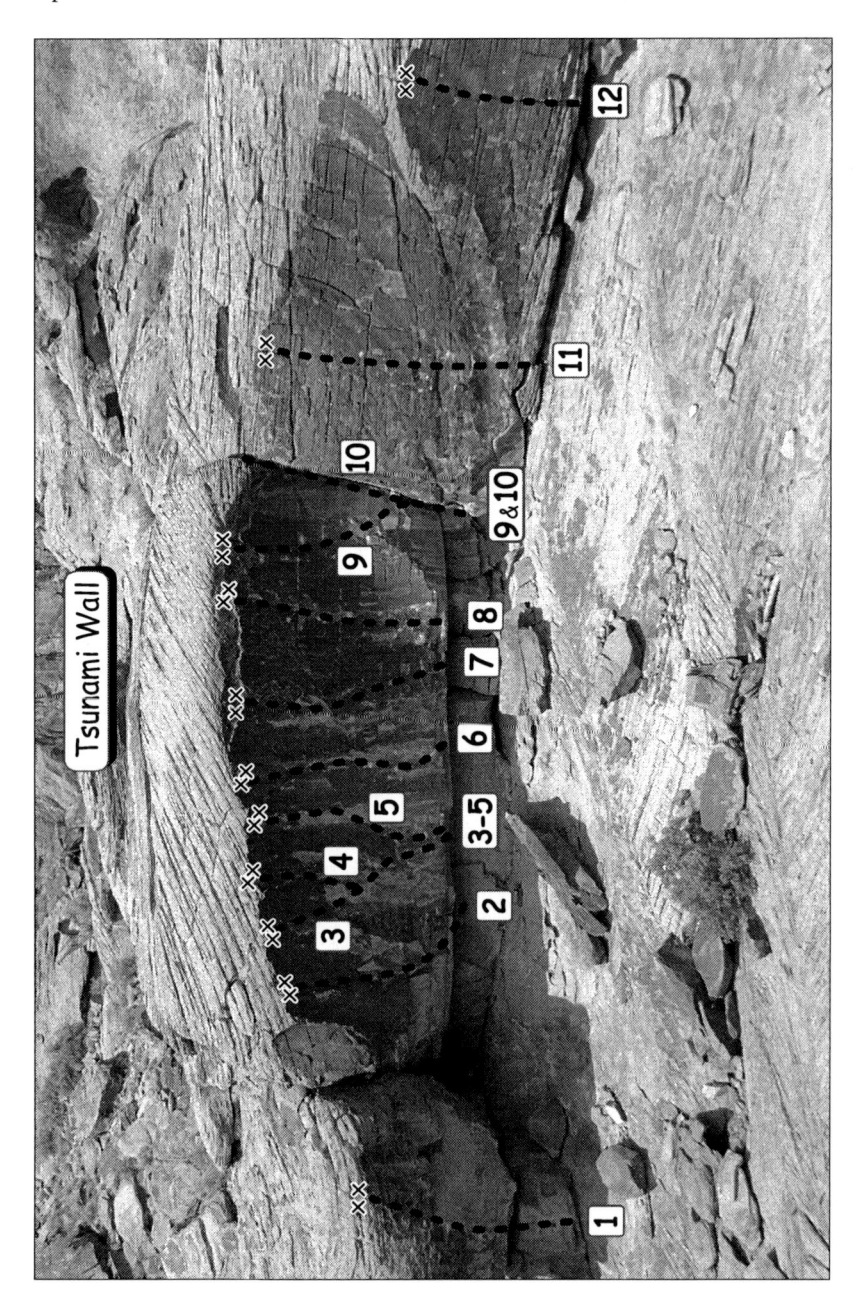

The Gallery

Probably the most popular sport-climbing crag at Red Rocks, The west-facing Gallery is littered with bolt routes and can be quite crowded on those perfect winter days. To reach The Gallery, follow the obvious trail towards the crag, crest over a small hill and head back down to the wash. Cross the wash at the obvious dead pine tree and head up the slabs to the wall. An easier approach is to access a skinny corridor at the bottom of the slabs below The Gallery wall after crossing the wash at the dead pine tree. Follow this wash up (left) until it dead ends into a small box-canyon, climb up and out of this corridor and circle right towards the cliff. If you follow the corridor you'll end up at the left side of the wall, if you scramble up the slabs you'll end up below the right side of the wall at its steepest point.

Liv Sansoz climbing in The Gallery   photo: Olivier Appourchaux

1. Range Of Motion 5.10d
Climb the leftmost route on the wall, through a pod, past four bolts.
2. Sport Climbing Is Neither 5.8
Climb the short S-crack 65 feet right of Range Of Motion past three bolts.
3. Buck's Muscle World 5.9
Use your huge muscles to crank your way past three bolts, ten feet right of the short S-crack.

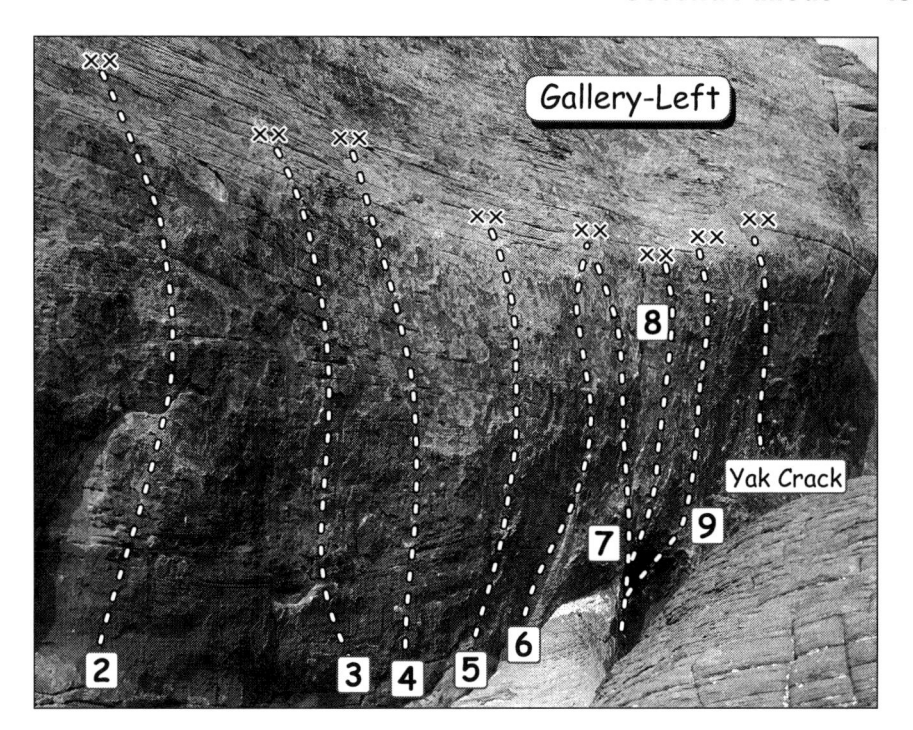

4. Gelatin Pooch 5.10a
Rope up eight feet right of Buck's Muscle World and climb past four bolts to anchors (three of these bolts have homemade hangers).
5. Pump First Pay Later 5.10b
Climb the next route right of Gelatin Pooch.
6. Running Amuck 5.10c
Start at the left-facing corner five feet right of Pump First Pay Later and crank your way up and right past four bolts.
7. Gridlock 5.11c
Start ten feet right of Running Amuck in the left side of the black pod and bust through the small holds up and left to the same anchors as Running Amuck.
8. Social Disorder 5.11d
Start in the same black pod but screw social order and climb straight up out of the pod past five bolts.
9. A Day In The Life 5.11b
Forget the humdrum—bust out the right side of the black pod past five bolts.
10. Minstrel In The Gallery 5.12b
Ten feet right of the black pod and just left of Yak Crack is this stellar route that climbs the steep face past five bolts.
11. Yak Crack 5.11d
Pump, grind and sidepull your way up this incredibly fun left-angling crack.

Gallery-right

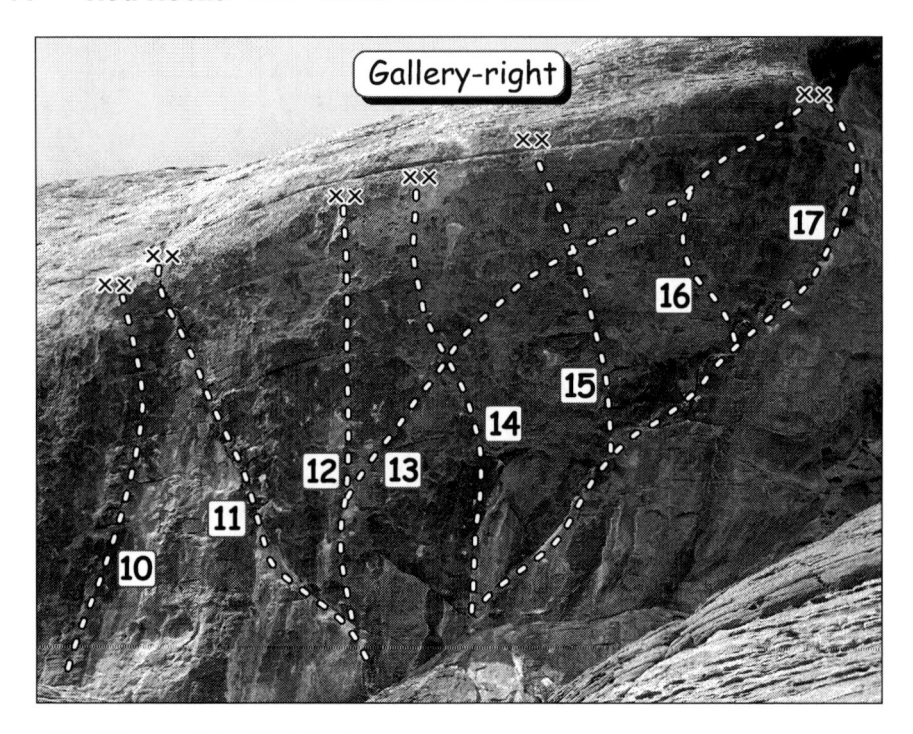

12. The Gift 5.12d
Start at the bottom of Yak Crack and crimp your way up tiny holds on this steep climb.

13. The Sissy Traverse 5.13b
Start as per The Gift but angle up and right, traversing across the wall to the Glitch anchors, while clipping black-painted bolts.

14. Where The Down Boys Go 5.12d
Just right of The Gift is a right-angling ramp. Start at the bottom of the ramp and head straight up past five bolts.

15. Who Made Who 5.12c
Clip the first two bolts heading up the ramp and then cut out left and straight up past three more bolts.

16. Nothing Shocking 5.13a
Start as per Who Made Who but continue right past one more bolt and then crank up and left past three more bolts to the anchor of Glitch.

17. Glitch 5.12c
Follow the aforementioned right-angling ramp to an obvious hueco and then head straight up to the anchors.

The Wall of Confusion

The Wall of Confusion is located at the far left end of The Gallery. You can't miss it—unless you're totally confused.

1. The Runaway 5.10b
Climb the furthest left route on the cliff past four bolts with homemade hangers.
2. American Sportsman 5.10c
Climb the four-bolt slab climb six feet right of The Runaway.
3. Desert Pickle 5.11b
Begin eight feet right of American Sportsman and climb the scary slab past four bolts.
4. Sudden Impact 5.11c
Crimp your way up the wall six feet right of Desert Pickle.
5. Big Damage 5.12b
Begin six feet right of Sudden Impact at the bottom of a right-leaning crack where the wall starts to get steep. Climb up and left around the roof and then back right through the upper roof.
6. Promises In The Dark 5.12b
Start under the obvious large roof six feet right of Big Damage and clip five bolts to anchors.
7. Fear And Loathing 5.12a
Start ten feet right of Promises and power your way up this incredibly steep rout past nine bolts.

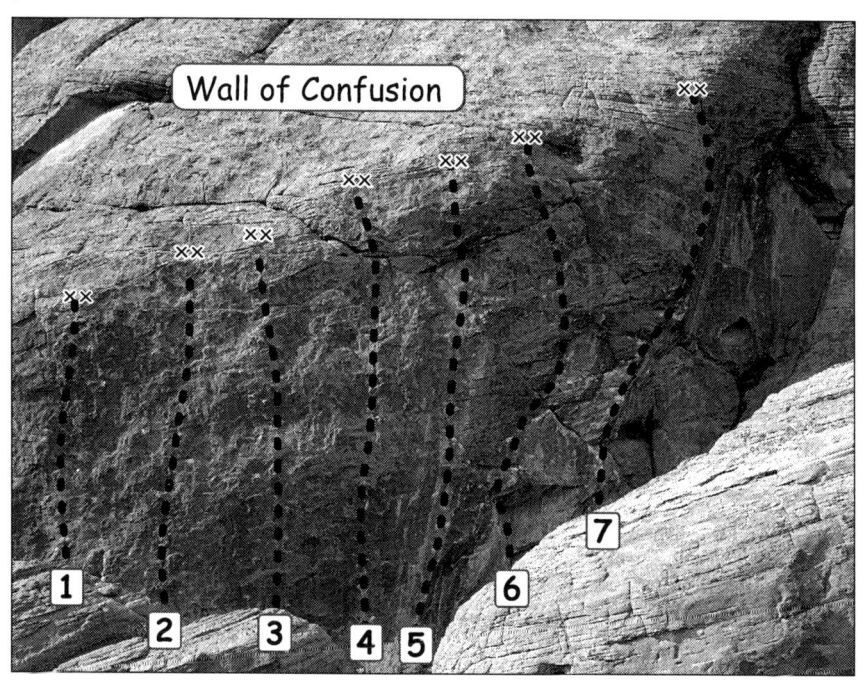

THIRD PULLOUT AREA AKA SANDSTONE QUARRY AREA
(SONIC YOUTH WALL, WAKE UP WALL, SATELLITE WALL, THE TROPHY)

The Sonic Youth Wall is a fantastic sport climbing crag that faces northeast, gets morning sun and is quite steep. The crag has two tiers and the best climbing is on the lower tier with its steep, overhanging routes. To reach Sonic Youth Wall, follow the trail out of the third pullout (Sandstone Quarry Parking lot) for about 200 yards until you reach an enormous white boulder (with awesome bouldering). Pass near by this boulder to the end of a small white cliff then hike the short steep trail to gain the top of the ridge on your left. Hike northwest along the top of this ridge for 1000 feet angling west but staying on the right side of the canyon in front of you. You will see the monolithic Broast And Toast Wall directly ahead of you on the right and Sonic Youth Wall is opposite this wall (facing north) on your left.

Sandstone Quarry Area Map

Third Pullout

Sonic Youth Wall

1. Hooligans 5.11c
This is the first route on the wall one will approach. Climb the leftmost bolt line straight up to a small bush.

2. GBH 5.11d
Rope up ten feet right of Hooligans and power through the big brown bulge. Escape left to the anchors of Hooligans after the sixth bolt.

3. Black Flag 5.11+
Start behind the bushes at the base of the black streak 20 feet right of GBH. Power up the left side of the black streak through the giant pod and walk off to the right.

4. Loki 5.12a
Crank up the right side of the black streak ten feet right of Black Flag until you hit a chain anchor after six bolts.

5. Agent Orange 5.12b
Everything turns gray on this seven- bolt rout that starts ten feet right and shares the same anchor as Loki.

6. Sonic Youth 5.11d
Rack up 20 feet right of Agent Orange at some huecos and bust up and left to a super-high first bolt.

7. Everybody's Slave 5.11c
Climb up the obvious steep black streak on the right side of the wall.

8. Crankenstein 5.10c
This runout route climbs the obvious black streak above Everybody's Slave and can top off any of the previous routes.

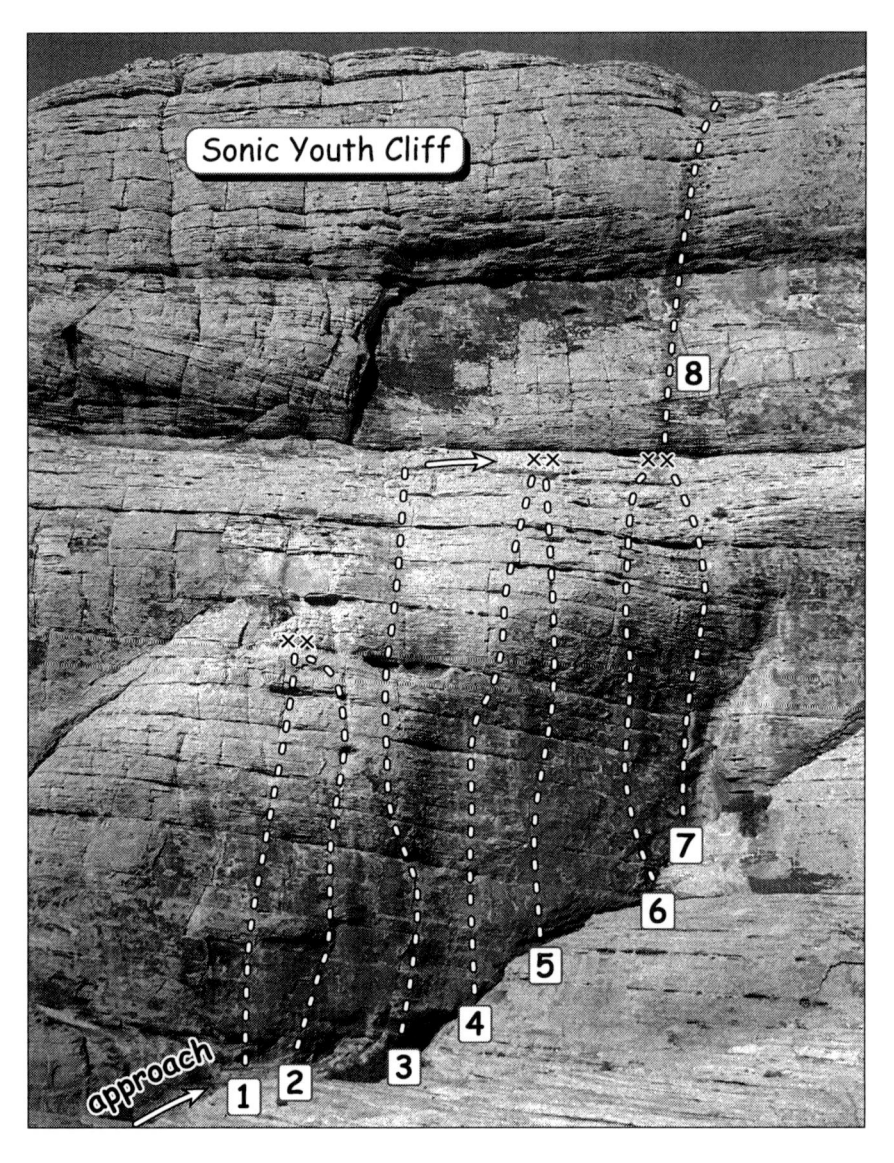

Red Rocks

Sonic Youth Cliff

THE WAKE UP WALL

The Wake Up Wall gets early morning sun in the winter and is nice and cool and shady in the summer. The wall is littered with short bolted lines mostly in the 5.11 and 5.12 range. To get to the Wake Up Wall hike north from the parking lot past a large white boulder in the main wash and gain an old road. Hike north along this road until you reach a sign that says Calico Tanks straight ahead and Turtlehead left. Take the trail left (west) and hike about two hundred yards, keeping a wash on your right.

WAKE UP WALL LEFT

1. First Born 5.10b
A great warm-up route just left of the enormous cave-like pod that makes Just Shut Up And Climb so rad.

2. Just Shut Up And Climb 5.11b
I don't want to hear it... By far the best route on the wall: steep jug hauling through the pod.

3. Unknown 5.10
Clip the bolts up the brown slab 30 feet right of Just Shut Up And Climb.

Wake Up Wall Right

Just right of the left-angling, right-facing corner that separates the wall is a schwaggy 5.11 bolt route with three homemade hangers. Don't bother.

4. The Healer 5.11d
Crimp your way up the left side of the brown scoop just right of the three homemade hangers.

5. Rise And Whine 5.12a
Stop your whining and bring me that coffee. Climb small holds on the right side of the aforementioned brown scoop to the anchors of The Healer.

6. Pain Check 5.12a
Ten feet right of Rise And Whine is another high-quality sport route with thin holds, hard moves and five bolts.

7. Good Mourning 5.11b
Climb the five-bolt line, ten feet right of Pain Check, up to a right-facing corner.

8. Native Son 5.11c
Start ten feet right of Good Mourning and crank your way past a hueco down low and five bolts.

9. Where Egos Dare 5.12a
If you have any sort of ego you would climb the steep pod that this route skirts left around.

10. XTC 5.9
Climb the left-angling slab/arete. Beware—the first bolt is missing.

11. Onsight Flight 5.12b
Rope up five feet right of XTC and just go for it!

12. Stand And Deliver 5.12b
Climb the steep five-bolt route directly right of Onsight Flight.

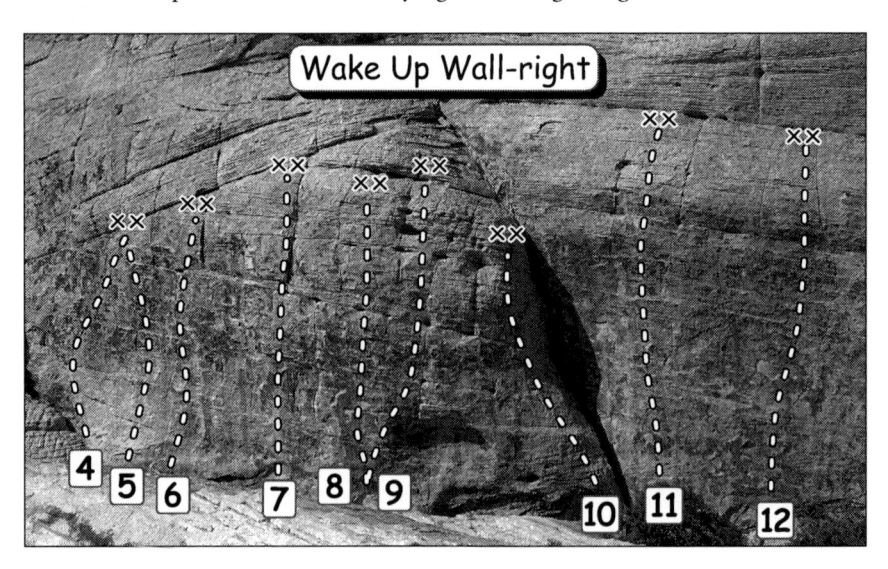

Third Pullout 51

The Satellite
The Satellite is an incredibly cool chunk of stone situated high on the cliffs across from the Wake Up Wall, offering great views, hard climbing on steep rock and a feeling of having the park all to yourself. To reach The Satellite follow the directions as for The Trophy but head south up the steep gully when you can see this wall.

1. Stargazer 5.12c
The leftmost route, with seven bolts, on the formation. If you like steep huecos jump on this rig and you'll be seeing stars.

2. Sputnik 5.12a
Just five feet right is the crag's warm-up route, checking in at 5.12a and climbing just left of the arete.

3. Supernova II 5.12c
One of the best 5.12s in Red Rocks, Supernova II climbs the steep face just right of the arete.

4. Cosmos 5.12d
A harder variation of Supernova II. Climb up and right after clip-

THE TROPHY

This wall is one of the best sport climbing venues in Red Rocks. The holds are positive, the bolts are well placed, the rock is steep (really steep!) and the crag basks in the sun for much of the day. All the routes here are 5.12 and 5.13 and require burliness and/or finesse. To access this cliff, hike north from the parking lot down across the wash and continue north on the main trail, keeping the wash on your right. After a couple of minutes you'll pass the Calico Tanks/Turtlehead sign (and trail heading left), continue straight 150 more yards until you run into a large wash that heads west on your left. Follow this wash west until you come across the picture below (or above). Then simply follow the trail up to the crag.

Trophy and Satellite area

1. Shark Walk 5.13a
Begin just right of the obvious cave and power up past six bolts.
2. Indian Giver 5.12c
Just right of Shark Walk is a thin and devious five-bolt route.
3. Unknown 5.12+
Climb the leftmost route on the main Trophy Wall past seven bolts to anchors.
4. Midnight Cowboy 5.13a
Boot, scoot and boogie your way up, angling left past five bolts and then straight up past three more bolts.
5. Twilight Of A Champion 5.13a
Rope up as per Midnight Cowboy but cut straight up after the third bolt.
6. Pet Shop Boy 5.12d
Begin ten feet right of Twilight Of A Champion and crank your way up the extremely steep face. Watch out for gerbils stuffed into pockets.

Third Pullout

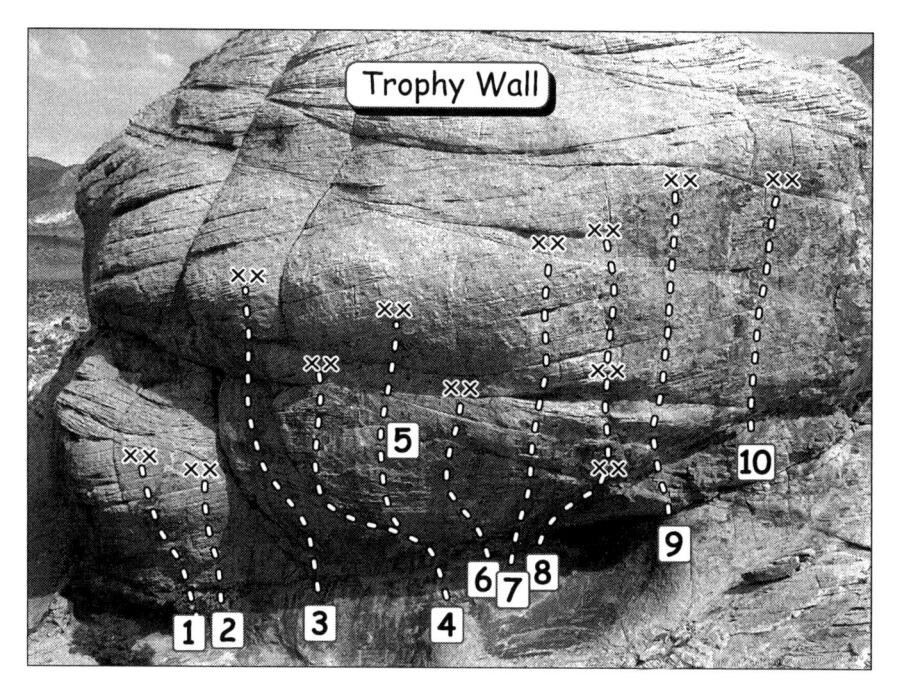

7. Keep Your Powder Dry 5.12d
Your powder will stay dry in this cave even in a downpour because it is so damn steep. 40 feet right of Pet Shop Boy, Clip the bolts on one of the longest and best routes on the wall.

8. The Trophy 5.12c
Follow the right-angling crack through the steep roof just right of Keep Your Powder Dry. There is a two-bolt anchor at the third bolt and at the sixth—I guess it just depends on how big you want your trophy to be.

9. Caught In The Crosshairs 5.12a
Set your sights on this route for a good warm-up.

10. Dodging A Bullet 5.12a
Another good long warm-up, 40 feet right of Caught In The Crosshairs.

WILLOW SPRING AREA

RAGGED EDGES
This is the obvious large black cliff on your left a half-mile after leaving the loop road. Park at the Willow Spring picnic area and cross the large wash and make your way up to the cliff. Be prepared to place some gear on some of these routes as well as clipping bolts.

1. Kemosabe 5.10b
Begin on the face just left of the obvious arch 100 feet left of Ragged Edges. Climb the incipient cracks past one bolt way up high and continue up the scary arete to the top. Either walk off to the right or rap off the small tree.

2. Tonto 5.5
Probably the best 5.5 you'll ever get-onto.

3. Vision Quest 5.12d
Begin just right of Tonto in the manky left-facing dihedral and power your way up and right over the steep wall. Rap at the anchors or continue up the wall (5.10).

4. Bodiddly 5.10+
Rope up around the corner from Vision Quest and climb the slab past very few bolts.

5. Plan F 5.11
If plans A-E don't work, climb the killer finger crack ten feet left of Ragged Edges. Either rap off the midway anchors of Ragged Edges or continue up and left past a couple bolts.

6. Ragged Edges 5.8
Nothing ragged about this climb. Climb the obvious varnished crack that splits the wall. A 60-meter cord helps get one to the belay tree.

7. Chicken Eruptus 5.10
Climb the right-angling white ramp five feet right of Ragged Edges and bust your way up through awesome solution pockets to the top.

8. Gun Boy 5.11+
You best be packin' some serious heat for this rig. Start 25 feet right of Chicken Eruptus at the shallow, rounded white dihedral and shoot your way up past one bolt into the darker dihedral to some sketchy moves on small gear and then a few more bolts. Walk off along the terrace to the right.

9. Sheep Trail 5.10c
Rope up ten feet right of Gun Boy at the obvious start and bust up through horizontal pockets to a left-facing corner. Continue up to the terrace and belay here utilizing small to mid-sized cams.

There are a few routes right of Sheep Trail but don't bother.

Willow Springs 55

Ragged Edges

LOST CREEK CANYON

The awesome Left Out Crag is located directly off the trail on the left near Hidden Falls. The routes on this crag ascend steep varnished faces and cracks and will have you saying "Wow! I'm glad this wasn't left out of the guide." To approach this crag park at the dirt pullout 0.2 miles off of the loop road at the Willow Creek turnoff. Follow the trail towards Hidden Falls for about 15-20 minutes. You'll see Left Out directly off the trail to your left behind a large boulder. Scramble up the left side of the boulder to the base of the climbs.

LEFT OUT CRAG

1. Killer Clowns 5.10d
Climb the ramp on the left side of the wall and then up through a difficult offwidth to easier cracks and face climbing above. Walk off the top of the cliff south and then down a fourth-class gully.

2. Left Out 5.10d
Climb the beautiful crack just right of Killer Clowns on the left side of the varnished main face. Exit as per Killer Clowns.
3. Right In 5.11b
Twenty feet right of the base of Left Out is a left-leaning crack that joins Left Out about 40 feet off the ground. Climb this.
4. Black Track 5.9
Just right of Right In is a kick-ass right-leaning crack that heads up to a chain anchor. Climb this.
5. Bigfoot 5.10a
Begin 25 feet right of Black Track and use your big feet to ascend the overhanging wall past four bolts to the Black Track anchors.
6. Buffalo Balls 5.11c
The cousin of the rocky mountain oyster? Clip the four bolts on the steep tan face right of Bigfoot.

Icebox Canyon

ICEBOX CANYON

Icebox Canyon can be reached by driving approximately eight miles on the scenic loop road and locating the Icebox Canyon parking area. A 20-25 minute hike up the Icebox Canyon Trail will deposit you directly in front of this spectacular chunk of stone. The following three routes ascend the heavily varnished, dark brown vertical buttress that is littered with cracks, both vertical and horizontal. All three routes utilize natural gear and share one anchor. Be prepared for some stiff climbing on stellar rock.

TARANTULA WALL

1. Gotham City 5.12a
This route climbs the right side of the face using the small crack for protection.

2. Spring Break 5.11d
Climb the center of the wall, once again using a small vertical seam for pro and then some horizontal cracks as well.

3. Tarantula 5.12a
Rope up at the left edge of the wall and creep your way up just right of the arete and then to the anchors.

Tarantula Face

BLACK VELVET CANYON

Black Velvet Canyon is one of the ultra-mega climbing areas in Red Rocks. It is home to classic multi-pitch routes, hard single-pitch routes, and excellent cracks, all on amazing rock. The approach is relatively easy and flat and will take you anywhere from 25 minutes (for Frogland) to 45 minutes (for Dream Of Wild Turkeys). The area is divided into three different buttresses; Frogland Buttress, Ixtalan Buttress and Black Velvet Wall.

To get to the trailhead you'll have to drive west on Hwy 160 just under five miles from the intersection with Hwy 159. Look for a large dirt road on your right with a cattle guard at the highway and an obvious parking area about 50 yards off the highway. If you reach the 16-mile marker sign on Hwy 160 you've gone too far. Follow this dirt road north (back towards Red Rocks) where at 1.4 miles you'll hit a triangular intersection—go straight. At 1.5, 1.7 and 1.8 miles you'll come across washes, again continue straight until you hit a steel gate at 1.9 miles where you'll be forced to go left. Follow this road a half-mile past closed parking areas on your left and about 30 seconds later you should be parking on your right. To reach the climbs follow the road towards the cliffs and then take the first obvious trail on your right (when the road goes left) that parallels the main wash coming out of the canyon.

FROGLAND BUTTRESS

To access this route follow the trail that parallels the main wash until you reach a fork just past some large boulders. Take the left trail heading up a steep hill and circumnavigating the band of red cliff up and to your right. This trail will bring you up to the base of Frogland.

1. Frogland 5.8

This is a classic six-pitch route near the mouth of the canyon. The first five pitches are each 150 feet long so bring lots of gear.
P1-Start at the white pillar at the base of a left-facing dihedral and climb past three bolts in this dihedral. Gain the highest ledge with oak bushes on it and belay here. 5.7
P2-Climb the awesome open-book dihedral up and right to a large ledge. Continue up another 70 feet to another ledge just below the huge bush. 5.6
P3-Crank a small roof and head left into the obvious dihedral. Pull over a bulge and head up and right to the bottom of a brown dihedral and belay here. 5.6
P4-Bust out left towards to a ledge below the white dihedral then climb this dihedral clipping one bolt and gaining the roof above. Traverse straight left to an arete then up the small crack. Continue up the corner systems to the next belay stance at the obvious bush. 5.8
P5-Make your way past one bolt up a slab to the main dihedral. Tunnel through the backside of the chockstone and then cut right over it and head past a white bulge to a beautiful chimney above. Belay at the base of the chimney. 5.8

P6-Climb the chimney and gain the awesome slab and climb the thin cracks up to a ceiling where you'll cut left to gain the next belay ledge with another bush on it. 5.6
P7-Make your way up to the top of the buttress via 100 feet of easy fourth class climbing.
Descent: From the top head east (climber's left) to the rightmost of three gullies down towards the road and then curl around the buttress back to the base of the climb.

descent

Frogland to Triassic Sands

Ixtalan Buttress
This amazing chunk of stone is 200 feet right of Frogland and can be approached the same way.

2. Kenny Laguna 5.10d
P1-Start in the short dihedral under the middle of the roof. Gain a weakness that heads right, turn the corner and head up to a belay stance.
P2-Climb the phat right-facing corner for 140 feet to rap anchors. Rap with two ropes to get safely back to the ground.

3. Return To Forever 5.10+
Rope up 100 feet right of Kenny Laguna and climb this three-pitch offwidth route. Rap the route.

4. Mazatlan 5.10+
Climb the obvious right-facing corner system up to an anchor below the roof.

5. Ixtalan 5.11c
P1-Start in the right-facing corner and clip four bolts in the corner, and then angle up and right clipping three more bolts to gain the obvious crack system.
P2-Continue 60 feet up the crack to a hanging belay.
P3-Crank through the stiff 5.11 roof to the anchor. Rap the route.

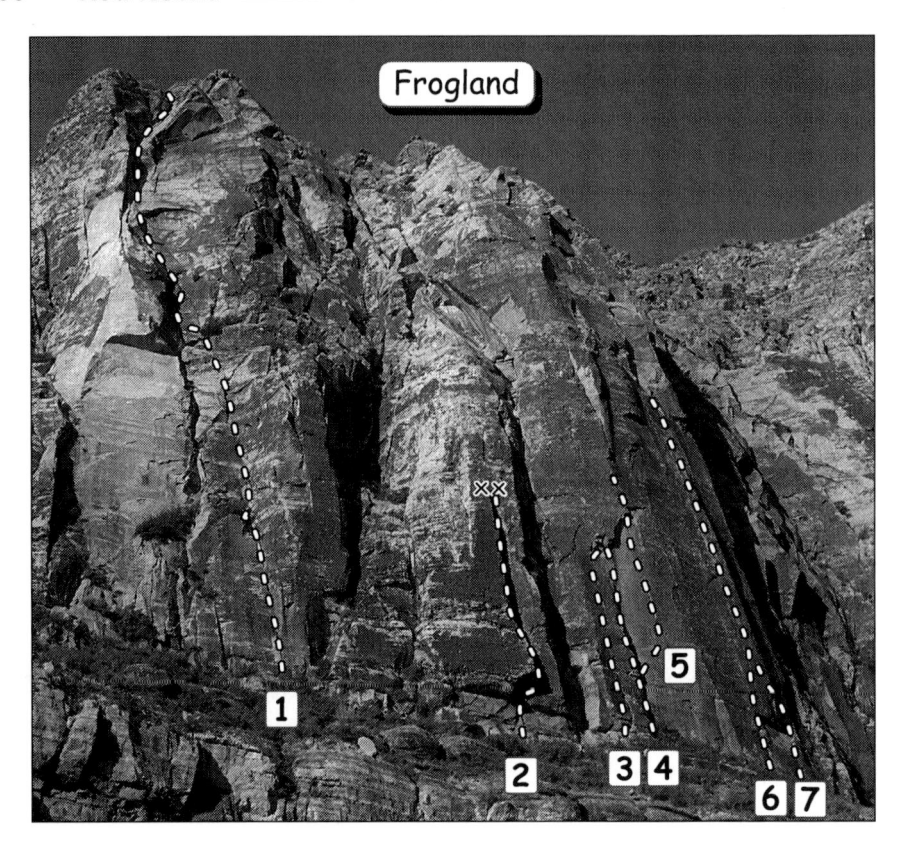

6. Triassic Sands 5.10
This three-pitch route is a must-do.
P1-Start 100 feet right of Ixtalan in a shallow, left-facing dihedral and climb this for 40 feet to the big ledge.
P2-Step left and gain the thin crack that heads up and left around the corner and climb this for 100 feet to some cold-shut anchors. 5.10
P3-Continue with fun crack climbing for another 160 feet up to a good ledge with rap anchors. Rap the route.

7. Cole Essence 5.11b
This can be done as a variation to Triassic Sands. Climb the striped dihedral from the big ledge atop the first pitch of Triassic Sands and rap off the route using anchors on the arete on the right.

BLACK VELVET WALL

This is the obvious enormous dark-brown wall located ten minutes up the canyon from Frogland, on the same side of the canyon. This wall gets very little sunshine, making it an ideal summer area but a frigid winter crag. Bring plenty of gear as the routes are long, the temps can change quickly and the climbing can be quite difficult.

To approach this wall, follow the road 1000 feet from the parking lot and take the obvious trail on the right where the road goes left. Follow this trail about 0.5 miles until it forks. The left goes to Frogland etc. Take the right fork down into the wash. Hike up the wash for about 500 yards until you can see the lower end of the small white cliffband at the base of the wall and the wash is impassable. Take the trail (left) up towards the right side of this cliffband and fourth class your way up the right side of the cliff via large ledges, then hike back left below the wall to the base of the routes. The routes are listed from left to right.

1. Rock Warrior 5.10

This sparsely bolted, runout six-pitch route will have even the solid 5.10 leader asking themselves why they engage in the silly and dangerous sport of rock climbing. However, the climb is excellent, and there will probably be nobody else on it. All of the pitches are 150 feet so be prepared with loads and loads of small gear and two ropes to retreat.
P1-Begin in the middle of the white rock 75 feet left of the huge arching roof. Climb up and right through scary moves past three bolts to the anchors. 5.10-
P2-Bust out left to a bolt and then head straight up to a left-facing corner and clip another bolt and climb the edge of the corner up to a thin crack up and right to the anchor. 5.10-
P3-Angle a little left from the anchor and head for the small roof. Crank out the roof to reach the anchor. 5.10
P4-Face climb for 150 feet to the anchor by a corner. 5.9
P5-More face climbing past the corner will get you past more bolts and up to another anchor. 5.9
P6-Pull the shallow roof and then crank through the cracks up to the last anchor. 5.10
Rappel the route.

2. The Prince of Darkness 5.10c

This route is just the opposite of Rock Warrior. Incredibly well protected, it will have the solid 5.10 leader wondering why there are so many bolts. But regardless, this is a great route with fabulous exposure and airy hanging belays—and rather popular. Bring two ropes for retreat.
P1-Rope up as per Dream of Wild Turkeys at the base of the obvious right-leaning dihedral 100 feet off the ground. Slab climb 75 feet up to a three-bolt anchor. 5.6
P2-Climb straight up for 110 feet passing a ridiculous number of bolts. 5.10

62 **Red Rocks**

Black Velvet Wall

P3-Once again chase the bolt line up for 130 feet. 5.10
P4-Hey, what a concept, climb for 125 feet clipping many, many bolts. 5.10
P5-Bust out left and then follow the bolted crack past (you guessed it) more bolts. 5.9
P6-Climb this crux pitch past 13 bolts on a varnished slab for 130 feet up to the anchors of Dream of Wild Turkeys.
Rappel the route.

3. Dream of Wild Turkeys 5.10
One of the all-time greatest classics in Red Rocks. Bring gear and plenty of quickdraws for this route and two ropes to retreat with.
P1-Begin at the same start as for Prince of Darkness and climb 75 feet up to the anchor. 5.6
P2-Cut right into the right-leaning dihedral and place some gear in the crack. 5.9
P3-Climb up a bit and then head right (Yellow Brick Road goes straight up here) while clipping bolts and then angling right and up to a white, right-facing corner. 5.9
P4-Climb the corner and then make some face moves past more bolts up to an anchor 165 feet above the last anchor. 5.10a
P5-Angle up and left for 50 feet while clipping bolts and head for a left-facing corner with belay anchors. 5.9+
P6-Scramble up and right following the left-facing corner until it ends. Head up via a small crack and then climb back right past more bolts to the anchors 140 feet above. 5.9
P7-Head straight up for 75 feet to reach the rap anchors. 5.9
You can keep going up, but why bother? Rap the route.

4. Yellow Brick Road 5.10
This is a three-pitch variation to Dream of Wild Turkeys. Climb the first two pitches of Dream and then head straight up past a plethora of yellow bolts for two pitches. (5.10a and 5.10c respectively) The third pitch climbs the left-facing flake past a couple of bolts and then rejoins Dream of Wild Turkeys.
Rap the route

5. The Gobbler 5.10a
This route climbs above the obvious right-arching roof on the right side of the wall.
P1-Start about 40 feet right of Dream of Wild Turkeys. Climb up and left past two bolts and then head right past a bolt and then up and left to an anchor on a ledge. 5.9
P2-Angle up and right through some cracks to a two-bolt belay. Either stop and belay here or head straight up past a few bolts to rejoin Dream.

6. Fiddler on the Roof 5.10+
This is an airy and exciting climb that will make you hope and pray you don't fall (if you do you'll be dangling). Bring gear and plenty of quickdraws for this pleasurable mixed route.
P1-Same start as The Gobbler. 5.9
P2-Stop at the midway belay station and take in the view. 5.9
P3-Head right just above the roof past a couple of bolts and some natural gear. (WHOA!!) 5.10-

P4-Head directly up, passing a few bolts and more gear placements, for 150 feet. 5.10c
P5-Ascend another 150 feet passing bolts and yet more gear placements to an anchor.
P6-Similar to the previous two pitches; 150 feet of mixed 5.10 climbing.
P7-Clip two more bolts to gain Turkey Ledge.
Rap Dream of Wild Turkeys with two ropes.

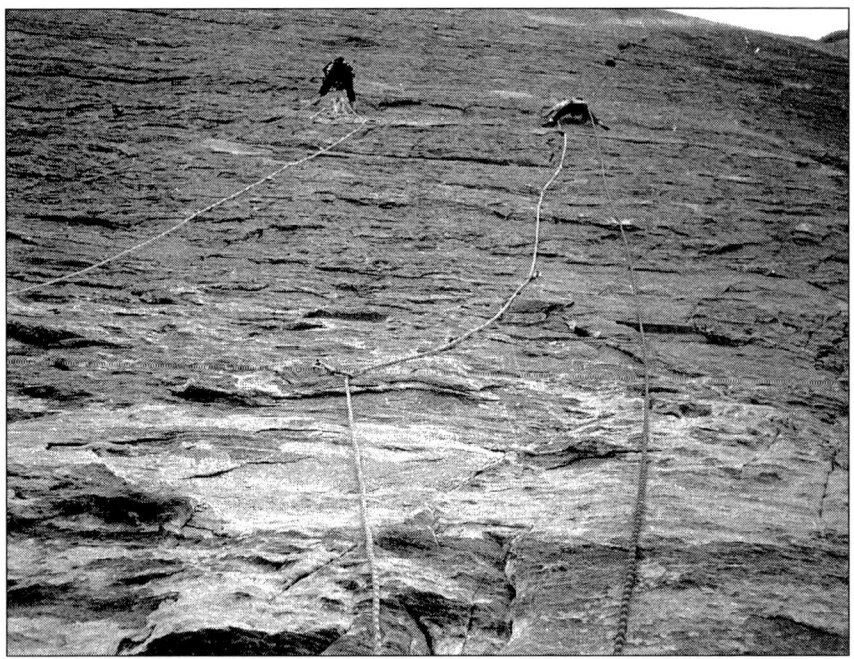

Climbers on Rock Warrior and Prince of Darkness

About the Author
Rob Floyd has climbed in Las Vegas for nearly fifteen years. He usually makes the road trip in the spring and/or fall trying to get in shape or to work on long-standing projects. A former freelance writer and climbing guide, Rob had the opportunity to travel at length and experience the diversity of many different climbing areas. He has contributed to Rock And Ice, Climbing and National Geographic's Adventure Magazine. He is now a medical doctor finishing his residency in Orthopedics.

DON'T MISS THE NEARBY CLIMBING MECCA OF ST. GEORGE, UTAH

The region around St. George, Utah is home to over 50 crags on seven diferent rock types. Rock Climbs of Southwest Utah and the Arizona Strip covers this plethora of quality climbing from the difficult limestone routes of the Virgin River Gorge to the family-friendly basalt of Crawdad Canyon to the multi-pitch sandstone classics in Spring Canyon, and much more...

TODD GOSS
SOUTHWEST UTAH & THE ARIZONA STRIP

Sharp End Publishing
Authentic Guides From Core Climbers

Now avilable— the new full-color 320 page

Rock Climbs of Southwest Utah and the Arizona Strip

Available at fine mountain shops or online at
www.sharpendbooks.com

Index

A
Abandon Ship 5.12a 39
Across The Universe 5.11c 20
Aftershock 5.12b 39
Agent Orange 5.12b 47
Almost Real 5.6 11
American Sportsman 5.10c 45
Animal Attack 5.12c 28
Animal Attack Extension 5.13b 28
Ashes To Ashes 5.13a 9

B
Barracuda 5.13b 39
Big Damage 5.12b 45
Bigfoot 5.10a 56
Black Flag 5.11+ 47
Black Track 5.9 56
Black Velvet Canyon 58
Black Velvet Wall 61
Bloodbath 1 5.12d 21
Bloodbath 2 5.12d 21
Bloodline 1 5.12b 26
Bloodline 2 5.12c 26
Blue Man 5.6 23
Bodiddly 5.10+ 54
Borderline 5.13a 26
Boyz In The Hood 5.12c 23
Buck's Muscle World 5.9 42
Buffalo Balls 5.11c 56

C
Cat Walk 5.10a 34
Caught In The Crosshairs 5.12a 53
Central Slabs 12
Charleston 5.10b 15
Chicken Eruptus 5.10 54
Civilized Fool 5.11b 11
Closing Down 5.14a 28
Cocaine Hotline 5.11 37
Cole Essence 5.11b 60
Collective Peace 5.12a 12
Compton Cave, The 28
Contamination 5.12a 9
Cop Killer 5.12a 22
Cop Killer Cave 21
Corrosion (second pitch) 5.13b 20
Corrosion 5.13a 20
Corrosion Cave 20
Cosmos 5.12d 51
Countdown To Armageddon 5.13c 9
Crack 5.11b 36
Crankenstein 5.10c 47
Cujo 5.11d 35
Cut Your Hair Sister 5.10d 23

D
Dark Side, The 5.12c 24
Day In The Life, A 5.11b 43
Desert Pickle 5.11b 45
Direct Hit 5.14a 20
Disconnect 5.10d 11
Dodging A Bullet 5.12a 53
Dog Wall, The 34
Doo Doo Love 5.9 15
Dream Of The Wild Turkeys 5.10 63

E
Edible Panties 5.10+ 37
Ed's Route 5.12a 9
Eight Ball 5.11 37
Endless Needs And Bloody Deeds 5.12c 24
Energizer 5.13a 28
Equalizer 5.13a 28
Everybody's Slave 5.11c 47
Exacto Blade 5.11d 13

F
Facile 5.14b 28
Fear And Loathing 5.12a 45
Fiddler On The Roof 5.10+ 63
Fighting For Peace 5.11c 12
First Born 5.10b 49
First Pullout 34
Fixx Cliff, The 36
Flying Pig 5.10c 12
Free At Last 5.13d 28
Free Base 5.11 36
Friendly Fire 1 5.11d 18
Friendly Fire 2 5.13a 19
Frogland 5.8 58
Frogland Buttress 58

G
Gallery, The 41
GBH 5.11d 47
Geezer, The 5.11b 37
Gelatin Pooch 5.10a 43
Ghetto Booty 5.14b 15
Ghetto Boyz 5.13c 15
Glitch 5.12c 44
Glowing For It 5.10d 9
Gobbler, The 5.10a 63
Good Mourning 5.11b 50

Index

Gorillas In The Mist 5.12d 15
Gotham City 5.12a 57
Grandma Beth 5.10d 23
Gridlock 5.11c 43
Ground Zero 5.12c/d 9
Gun Boy 5.11+ 54
Gun Tower 1 5.12a 21
Gun Tower 2 5.12c 21
Gun Tower 3 21

H
Hasta La Manana 5.14b/c 28
Hasta La Vista 5.14b 28
Healer 5.11d, The 50
Heatin' Up The Hood 1 5.11c 22
Heatin' Up The Hood 2 5.11d 22
Heatin' Up The Hood 3 5.12a 22
Here Kitty, Kitty 5.11c 35
Honest Politician 5.11c 12
Hood, The 14
Hoodlum 5.12a 26
Hooligans 5.11c 47
Hyper Soul 5.14a 26

I
Icebox Canyon 57
Imagination Wall 9
Imaginator 5.11c 12
Indian Giver 5.12c 52
Infectious Booty 5.14b 16
Infectious Cave 15
Infectious Groove 5.13b 16
It's A Bitch 5.10b 34
Ixtalan 5.11c 59
Ixtalan Buttress 59

J
Jazz Ma Tazz 1 5.12c 23
Jazz Ma Tazz 2 5.13b 23
Just Shut Up And Climb 5.11b 49

K
K-9 5.12b 35
Keep Your Powder Dry 5.12d 53
Kemosabe 5.10b 54
Kenny Laguna 5.10d 59
Killer Clowns 5.10d 55

L
Land Shark 5.12b 39
Left Out 5.10d 56
Left Out Crag 55
Legend 5.14a 28
Legend Of The Overfiend 5.14b 28

Loki 5.12a 47
Lost Creek Canyon 55
Low Tide 5.10 40

M
Malt Liquor Man 5.11a, 5.11c 21
Man Overboard! 5.12d 39
Man's Best Friend 5.10 35
Mazatlan 5.10+ 59
Midnight Cowboy 5.13a 52
Minstrel In The Gallery 5.12b 43
Mo Betta 5.12b 23
Molotov Cocktail 5.13a 16
Mt. Charleston 7

N
Native Son 5.11c 50
Nothing Shocking 5.13a 44

O
Old World Order 5.11d 11
Onsight Flight 5.12b 50

P
Pain Check 5.12a 50
Panty Line 5.10a 38
Panty Raid 5.10 37
Panty Wall, The 37
Perfect World 5.12a 12
Pet Shop Boy 5.12d 52
Plan F 5.11 54
Poodle Chainsaw Massacre 5.11c 35
Poseidon Adventure 5.12b 39
Primal Soul 5.14a 26
Prince Of Darkness, The 5.10c 61
Project 5.? 26
Promises In The Dark 5.12b 45
Pump First Pay Later 5.10b 43

Q
Quark Corner 5.11b 9

R
Ragged Edges 54
Ragged Edges 5.8 54
Range Of Motion 5.10d 42
Rappin' Boyz 1 5.12a 23
Rappin' Boyz 2 5.12c 23
Reach The Beach 5.11 37
Red Rocks 31
Red Skies 5.11b 36
Repaginator 5.10+? 12
Return To Forever 5.10+ 59
Ricochet 5.12d 21
Right In 5.11b 56

Index

Rise And Whine 5.12a 50
Rock Warrior 5.10 61
Run For The Border 5.13b 26
Run For The Border Extension 5.13d 26
Runaway, The 5.10b 45
Running Amuck 5.10c 43

S
Sandstone Quarry Area 46
Sattelite, The 51
Saved By Zero 5.11 36
Screaming Target 5.13c 20
Second Pullout 39
Selective War 5.11a 12
Self-Destruct Sequence 5.12a 9
Shark Walk 5.13a 52
Sheep Trail 5.10c 54
Shit Jaws 5.12b 28
Short But Stout 5.12c 20
Silk Panties 5.7 38
Sissy Traverse, The 5.13b 44
Slaughterhouse 5.12b 15
Snow Blind 5.11 R 36
Social Disorder 5.11d 43
Sonic Youth 5.11d 47
Sonic Youth Wall 47
SOS 5.13a 39
Soul Man 5.13d 26
Soul Train 5.14a 26
South Central Slabs 23
Sport Climbing Is Neither 5.8 42
Spring Break 5.11d 57
Sputnik 5.12a 51
Stand And Deliver 5.12b 50
Stand Or Fall 5.11a 36
Stargazer 5.12c 51
Straight Outa Compton 5.12d/13a 28
Straight Outa Compton/Animal Attack 5.13b/c 28
Sudden Impact 5.11c 45
Supernova II 5.12c 51

T
Tarantula 5.12a 57
Tarantula Wall 57
Test Site, The 9
The Angler 5.12c 39
The Gift 5.12d 44
Third Pullout Area 46
Threadfin 5.12c 39
Tonto 5.5 54
Toprope 5.12a 23

Totally Clips 5.11+ 37
Tremor 5.10 40
Triassic Sands 5.10 60
Trophy, The 52
Trophy, The 5.12c 53
Tsunami Wall, The 39
Twilight Of A Champion 5.13a 52

U
Unknown 5.10 49
Unknown 5.10+ 11, 37
Unknown 5.10a 38
Unknown 5.10c 13
Unknown 5.11 12
Unknown 5.11c 13
Unknown 5.12+ 52
Unknown 5.12a 37
Unknown 5.13+? 9
Unknown 5.13a 9
Unknown 5.9 15
Urban Decay 5.12c 16

V
Vision Quest 5.12d 54

W
Wailing Souls Cave 26
Wake Up Wall Left 49
Wake Up Wall Right 50
Wake Up Wall, The 49
Walk By Slab 18
Wall of Confusion, The 45
Warlord 5.13a 20
Where Egos Dare 5.12a 50
Where The Down Boys Go 5.12d 44
Whiff, The 5.10a 36
Who Made Who 5.12c 44
Willow Springs Area 54
Wired 1 5.12c 23
Wired 2 12c 23
Wired 3 5.12c 23
Witness This! 5.13b 22
Witness To A Killin' 1 5.11b 22
Witness To A Killin' 2 5.10d 22
Witness To A Killin' 3 5.12b 22
Witness To A Killin' 4 5.12c 22
Women And Children First 5.7 39

X
XTC 5.9 50

Y
Yak Crack 5.11d 43
Yellow Brick Road 5.10 63